The time is ripe to crea⎵⎵⎵⎵⎵⎵⎵⎵ Champions in Vietnam. ⎵⎵⎵⎵⎵⎵⎵⎵⎵ entrepreneurs as well as those who work hard to put 91 million Vietnamese on the global agenda. Reading this book gives a better understanding why there is no future without understanding the diversity and wealth of Asean thinking.

Roland Schatz
Founder of Media Tenor, Zurich, Switzerland
Co-author, *The Global President: International Media and the US Government*

Every story in the book is so beautifully written. Once I started reading it, I could not put it down until the last page. The authors used true stories of their personal life experience and that of others, from their early childhood days and how those experiences shaped their lives. Most of those real personalities are successful today.

By cleverly weaving these simple story lines, the authors raise some very provocative questions. Readers will find the stories and the questions irresistibly attractive and inspiring. But most importantly, behind each story, readers will get a vivid impression of the actor's inner thought, his emotion, his vision, his laughter, and sometimes his tears. Their stories mirror the aspirations and hope of the ordinary Vietnamese that you may come face to face with on the streets in the country.

With these stories, the writers see hope. They seek to share their views and perhaps offer an answer about how to navigate the critical pathways that can lead the nation to great prosperity.

A fascinating book.

Loke Kiang Wong
Retired Captain Singapore Navy
Singapore Navy and Contributor to Vietnamica.net

What we see, why we worry, why we hope provides valuable insight into the Vietnamese mindset. Useful for a student, traveler or businessperson, the anecdotes provide an insider's view into Vietnamese culture and its impact on the country's role in a dynamic region. Like Napier and Hoang, Stratfor holds a lot of hope for Vietnam as it transitions in a "post-China" era. Revealing anecdotes, woven throughout the authors' hopes and worries, offer a critical bridge for understanding a culture shaped by unique geopolitical circumstances, highlighting both the challenges and opportunities for Vietnam's future. In a chaotic world, Napier and Hoang are able to explore the essence of Vietnam in simple but compelling snapshots, providing critical insights for Vietnam's future.

George Friedman
Chairman, Stratfor
Author of *The Next Decade* and *The Next 100 Years*

So rich in real life stories that the book makes you "live Vietnam." The book elegantly weaves the past with the present, daily life with reflections, and the local with the global through the sharp observations by the authors.

Olav Jull Sørensen
Professor
Aalborg University, Denmark
Medal of Honor Recipient
Vietnam's Ministry of Education and Training

A cogent and compelling look at contemporary Vietnam with all its complexities and contradictions. Vuong Quan Hoang and Nancy Napier have given us a well-written and accessible guide to understanding the changes that Vietnam has gone through in the last decade. This book will be of great use to anyone wanting to understand Vietnam today.

Anya Schiffrin
Columbia University's School of International and Public Affairs
(Co)Author of *From Cairo to Wall Street: Voices from the Global Spring* and *Bad News: How America's Business Press Missed the Story of the Century*

We – Vietnamese entrepreneurs and businesspeople – who have the wish of making Vietnam a better place to work and live have both worries and hopes for our home country. The authors have done a nice job of presenting a new Vietnam, a multi-colored society and an emerging market economy, with simple and fun-to-read style. The book delivers many important messages to western readers and we highly appreciate the great efforts by the authors trying to bring Vietnam to the world, and the world to Vietnam.

Vu Quang Hoi
Chairman
The Bitexco Group

WHAT WE
SEE
WHY WE
WORRY
WHY WE
HOPE

Việt Nam Going Forward

WHAT WE SEE WHY WE WORRY WHY WE HOPE

Việt Nam Going Forward

Nancy K. Napier ★ Vuong Quan Hoang

CCI PRESS
BOISE STATE UNIVERSITY

PUBLISHED BY CCI PRESS
Boise State University

Managing Editor: Stephanie Chism
Production Manager: Joanna Lui

ISBN 13: 978-0-9855305-8-7

CCI Press - http://cobe.boisestate.edu/cci/cci-press/
http://cobe.boisestate.edu/cci/vietnamgoingforward
All trademarks are the property of their respective companies.

Dedications

From VQH: To Thu Ha, Thu Trang and Ha My who have taught me what a love for the country and home can mean.

From NKN: To HSN and AWO, who first introduced me to Vietnam and, like the Vietnamese people, always forgive, make friends with so many, and look to the future.

TABLE OF CONTENTS

Foreword

This is an excellent book from which to learn about the real changes happening in Vietnam, a country that is experiencing one of the most rapid economic growth periods in the world, and is undergoing a radical change in its society. The book includes a very vivid description of the "bridge generation"—the generation, a group that bridges the old communist era and the free market era of the current transition economy. This generation knows both the Vietnam War (or as the Vietnamese say, The American War) and the *Doi Moi* economic reforms, which began in the 1980s. Of the people interviewed for the book, some were successful in business, while others failed repeatedly and eventually succeeded. Readers will be impressed by the stories about these and others described in the book.

Napier and Hoang describe the socio-economic challenges which Vietnam is facing. Readers' understanding of the book would be enhanced by some knowledge of the history behind the country's economic reforms. For example, the reform of state owned enterprises (SOEs) has been pursued with a philosophy "gradualism" and Vietnam initiated its agricultural reforms in the 1980s, and its opening to foreign trade in the 1990s.

I anticipate that this book will not only contribute to the general public's understanding of Vietnam, but also stimulate academic interests. If we look at countries and regions in East Asia, those with a Confucian background have achieved solid economic development. Japan, Korea, and China all have strong Confucian backgrounds, and their entrepreneurs are often influenced by Confucian ideas. Vietnam has a cultural and historical background that is similar to those

East Asian countries and regions. When Vietnam develops further, its corporations and entrepreneurs will need a corporate identity that will support their stability. I wonder where the Vietnamese corporations will find solutions. Whether they can successfully build their corporations based on a mix of Vietnamese socio-cultural values and emerging Western ideas of development remains a difficult question.

Junichi Mori
Vice President for International Relations
Director & Professor
The International Center, Kyoto University

Introduction

What We See, Why We Worry, Why We Hope: Vietnam Going Forward

The Vietnamese are humble and boastful. The Vietnamese are patient and love to gamble. They "swallow their insides" and take humiliation. We are like water buffalo— hardworking, not aggressive, obedient, and patient. But when provoked, watch out. When the water buffalo is pushed over some limit, it goes crazy, and can be very dangerous. Nothing will stop it. The Vietnamese people are the same—patient, hardworking, but if pushed, they'll push back.

Senior Vietnamese business manager

Every summer, Ms. Nam Phuong goes camping in the outskirts of Hanoi, far enough from the city to be among trees, close enough to town that the trip doesn't tire her fellow campers. Phuong and a colleague from her consulting firm take several eleven-year-old children of her other colleagues for an exciting and memorable two-night experience. The children are not too young and not too old. They've found that, for this experience, this age is just right.

During the first afternoon, the kids learn how to build a village. They collect wood, design structures and build small huts to make a village around a fire pit. They play in the village, deciding who will live where, who is the village chief, and how the others fit into their new society. They make dinner, tell stories like campers anywhere, and settle in for the night, anticipating one more fun day. But Phuong and her colleague know something the children do not.

The next morning the children awake to destruction. Their village, built with such pride and fun, is gone. The wooden huts lie collapsed in heaps and piles of splintered wood. The few belongings that the children brought have been ripped from their backpacks, torn to shreds, and lie dirty on the ground. Nothing is useable. The children stand around, mouths open, looking to the adults for answers.

The two women are volunteers in the CISV program (formerly known as the Children's International Summer Villages), a group that educates children about peace. The women ask the children how they feel about their destroyed village. Devastated, of course. So the women carefully talk through what they know from real experience and what the children are learning through this simulated one.

"This is Vietnam's history. Over and over, our villages have been destroyed by war, in fighting. Invaders kill our people, our families, take our belongings and our food. Our villages burn or collapse. It happens so often and peace comes so rarely that we must always prepare for the destruction of war. We may have peace for a few decades but do not get soft. War will come again, sometime. Always, always be ready."

But they also help children understand that just as they feel sad about their village, they need to remember that others would feel the same. So they urge them to remember those feelings and try to think about not destroying others' villages, but rather to work toward peace.

Then the children rebuild the village during the day. But they do so with limited resources, since so much was destroyed, and in the process they learn that it becomes even harder to build their dream village. Still, the children try to build a sturdier one. They talk about who should be guards and stay awake at night and how to fight off invaders the next time. Then, with visions of destruction and unpredictability burned into their memories, they return home.

WoW!

*

* *

Like many Vietnamese his age, Nguyên Trong Khang was a child, living in Hanoi during the "Christmas Bombings" in December 1972. When the American War in Vietnam ended three years later, his family was destitute, having little food, no electricity, and few possessions. But Khang remembers it a bit differently. "We had temporary peace," he said, "no guns, no fighting, no fear." Sadly, the temporary peace didn't last long. The Cambodian and Chinese Wars, long years of little food and later the collapse of the Soviet Union held Vietnam in a state of poverty and for some, outright famine. The Vietnamese lost lifelines of supplies, access to jobs and education and the economy continued to sink.

"But we tried to be positive," Khang said. "Maybe the ability to confront problems makes our people and our country always keep positive. Nothing is free. You get what you are today with a lot of sweat, pain and love."

Khang saw education as a road out of hardship, so he invested in himself, even when the price was exorbitant. In 1996, he used about two thirds of his total savings to pay an $8,100 fee to attend the Henley Management College postgraduate business program. And he paid in cash. After a year, he transferred to another masters level program, gaining admission to an American masters of business program, which included six months living in the U.S.

> *Before I went to America, I had a wife, a son and a house. All of the things that Vietnamese want in life. But when I was in the U.S., I saw universities and the power of having an education and how people start business. Instead of saving money for a bigger house, I save money for my son. I want my son to study abroad, to study in America.*

And that is exactly what happened 15 years later.

*
* *

With some entrepreneurs, you toss out an idea, press yourself against the wall to stay out of the way and watch what happens. We should have seen it coming with Khang.

On campus, the American university issued all students an identity card, but this one was unlike any Khang had seen—a card with a programmed chip that gave him access to worlds he didn't have in Vietnam—the gym, the library, the cafeteria. Khang loved its simplicity and potential. The card opened up possibilities to him and set the course of his business career.

He wrote about the story in a company brochure years later.

Hanoi, 2005

> MK Smartcards has been growing and expanding continuously for the past 6 years since the establishment of the company in 1999. The idea for MK business began with my student ID card when I was doing my MBA in the United States. It was not just an ID card as I could use it to pay for my meals at the cafeteria, to

borrow books at the library, be entitled to discounts at many shops... I started the card business right after coming back to Vietnam after finishing my MBA in 1999.

Khang has moved far beyond ID cards into smart cards (credit and debit cards, ePassports), mobile banking and secured transactions. His factories are among the few worldwide allowed to make Visa/Master cards and telephone SIM cards. He also created a mobile phone app that lets people add minutes to their phone credit, as well as send and receive money and pay bills online.

In fact, Khang is a sort of poster boy for Vietnamese entrepreneurship. His firm has received over $5 million in venture capital funds and it was highlighted in a Harvard Business School case and Khang was recently a finalist for Vietnam's Entrepreneur of the Year. Despite the notoriety, he is disconcertingly low key. He wears understated clothes and no jewelry, has a 4WD Toyota and driver (not a Range Rover or Mercedes, which many men in his situation might choose). His one extravagance seems to be collecting and refurbishing old Citroen cars, which he drives down the highway at a 30 MPH clip. You can imagine Catherine Deneuve in *Indochine*, without the rain.

And he works hard for it all. His partners are in Russia and South Africa, Korea and France. He's started and grown five companies in the last 13 years; he sits on boards of directors; he blends a global curiosity and ability to pick up on technology with an understanding of the local market, of what the Vietnamese are ready to accept and when.

Throughout, Khang has held firm to a philosophy that carries him forward.

"As Buddha teaches – 'give first – take later.' I built up a spirit and believe that 'money is not all' to guide me and my behavior, my style in the business. I feel proud to create jobs for people. I feel proud that I help make 'Made-in-Vietnam' products sitting in the wallets and mobile phones of 50 million Vietnamese... Interesting for me, maybe more than the money. Maybe I am a socialist – maybe not – but my next job is to help and empower other entrepreneurs in Vietnam to serve the market, create more job opportunity, encourage learning experience, and create a momentum of entrepreneurship spirit."

Khang's fifteen year old son spent a summer at Khang's alma mater university, studying English and learning about the U.S., and experiencing a 4th of July picnic and fireworks.

Meet the new Vietnam.

*

* *

These two short stories—of kids camping and an entrepreneur's awakening—illustrate the forces that are changing and challenging Vietnam. On the one hand, because some 60 % of young Vietnamese have never known war, older people worry that they will become soft, too trusting, and not stay resilient and resourceful when times become tough again, which they fear. On the other hand, Vietnamese in Khang's generation personally experienced the devastation of war as well as the new transition to a market economy and all that it can bring. Both stories show what is happening in Vietnam, some of the issues of concern, and yet the elements that will continue to bring hope and success for the country. With this book, we wish to raise questions and share insights that we hope will help both Vietnamese and Americans understand each other and some of their perspectives just a bit more than they may have yesterday.

Why this book now?

A quick click on Amazon.com for books about Vietnam can take your breath away. Over 30,000 books about Vietnam are available. So why one more? Largely, because of people like the children rebuilding a village, because of people like Khang and because of the many Americans who may think of "Vietnam" still as a war rather than a country, or who have no thoughts of Vietnam at all. If the people of Vietnam and America are to understand each other in the future, or even become partners economically and otherwise, we need to know more about the world that Khang and the children inhabit and how it is changing.

Americans who knew Vietnam as "the war" may be surprised to learn how many Vietnamese are like Khang or want to be like him. Khang is part of what we call "the bridge generation"—Vietnamese who grew up during the American War (or as Americans say, "the Vietnam War"). They suffered the hardships of war, recovery and rebuilding, and lost strategic allies when the Soviet Union collapsed. In the 1990s and 2000s, Vietnam then went through one of the most dramatic growth periods in its 2,000 year history, jolting and in some cases stumbling from a planned to market economy. Those Vietnamese who knew America as "the enemy" are fewer and soon even they will no longer exist. More often these days, Vietnamese are like the eleven year olds or their teenage siblings who know the U.S. as a place where movies and music, Nike and Apple come from.

Vietnam is a start-up country with a 2,000 year history (some would say 4,000 years, albeit not "recorded") but the change in the last twenty-five years has been more dramatic than in the previous 2,000. It has moved from desperate poverty and near famine in the late 1970s and early 1980s to one of the world's fastest growing economies, which in recent years has faced new challenges of sustaining such wild growth. Granted, it started from a small base but still, by the late 1990s, some considered Vietnam to be a potential "little tiger," following in the footsteps of Thailand or Malaysia. Unfortunately, that tiger never really roared.

In the last five years, the economy has flat-lined. Some sectors—like real estate—went into free fall in the 2011-2013 period. Managers of state owned enterprises (SOEs) too often appear in the news, accused of financial irregularities or doling out jobs to favored relatives or friends. Shifts in regulations and policy seem arbitrary at times and confusing at others. Their frequency and magnitude can give an observer whiplash. It's been a wild ride.

Vietnam is at a fork in its road toward development. Some Vietnamese leaders fear that the people are losing their way, forgetting to believe in themselves, and becoming too drawn into other approaches and temptations from countries far beyond their borders. Others are like Dang Lê Nguyên Vu, CEO of Trung Nguyên Coffee and known by some as Vietnam's "coffee king," who has built a thriving commercial enterprise and now is raising uncomfortable questions that also nudge people to consider where Vietnam's future will be. He wants to help Vietnam develop prosperously and sustainably and, with any person he meets—Vietnamese or foreign, long time friend or new acquaintance—Vu pushes the topic. What are the barriers to development? Are the Vietnamese cultural features of collectivism, hierarchy, face and short term thinking going to help or hinder the country going forward? Big and serious questions.

Yet despite the challenges, we—and many others—are optimistic and hopeful about Vietnam's future. We would like nothing more than to see the country roar. And some signals, perhaps weak but growing, hint at a bright future. First, people of the bridge generation, like Khang, are moving into leadership positions. Because they grew up during the wars in the 1970s and 1980s and have participated in the lurches toward a market economy, this group of Vietnamese understand both the hard and good times and many want to encourage the good parts of change.

In addition, we see some key characteristics that the Vietnamese people have exhibited for years and will serve them in the future—resourcefulness, resilience, and reinvention. To that end, some schools, companies, and parents are nurturing creativity in younger people, which will help boost development and integration into the broader world. Some of the country's key leaders show a generosity of spirit and ability to learn from failures. They are the ones who may help create new models for business and government and offer ideas and methods for what may be possible. So it makes sense to step back, take a look at some aspects of Vietnam today, what might be worrisome going forward, and what could help the country move to a positive future.

The book's title raises three questions that appear deceptively simple: What we see in Vietnam, what worries us, and why we are hopeful. They sound simple, but we've discovered, of course, they are not. As we asked others these questions, we found that even some of the most brilliant people who care about Vietnam's fate also find these questions difficult. One was Professor Dam Thanh Son, a University of Chicago physics professor. In early 2013, in response to a call from the Communist Party of Vietnam for opinions on reforming the constitution, Professor Dam and another well-known Vietnamese professor, Ngô Bao Châu, who won the Fields Medal (usually known as "Nobel Prize in Mathematics"), launched a website "Writing the constitution together" at http://hienphapnet.[1] Yet, when we asked the three questions, he readily acknowledged their importance but then declined to answer since he felt they deserved much more thought and time than he had available. He worried that his answers would not be helpful. His response helped us realize that the questions are not at all simple even for Vietnamese intellectuals.

Why us?

Vietnam has been the focus of so many books by so many authors—journalists, travel experts, former soldiers on both sides, refugees, professors—the list is long and many of the books and authors are prominent. So why us?

First, it's hard to find a book co-written by people from Vietnam and the U.S. that tries to incorporate both perspectives. Second, although we may see Vietnam from different viewpoints, we have many common beliefs, especially our love for Vietnam and its people, and our desire to see it succeed.

So who are we?

Hoang is an insider's insider and exemplifies the bridge generation. When we met, Hoang was an aggressive finance whiz working at a foreign bank in Hanoi. He then participated in the Masters in Business Administration program that Nancy ran through her university, and as part of the process, did an internship in the U.S. at a small business development center. Years later, he claimed that he learned only "one thing" while he was in the U.S. His big

---

[1] François Guillemot (2013) Ecrivons ensemble la constitution : une initiative vietnamienne constructive. *Sciences de l'Homme et de la Société, Mar. 24.* <http://halshs.archives-ouvertes.fr/halshs-00804959/>

lesson was "entrepreneurship," as a concept and as a way of thinking. He watched entrepreneurs come to the small business center and talk about ideas they had to start up a business. He watched other entrepreneurs return week after week for advice on how to run a business. Finally, Hoang saw entrepreneurs come to the center with stories of failure but energy to learn from the failure and start again. The attitude, the energy and the optimism struck him as something different from what he'd seen in Vietnam's planned economy but he realized that's what the country—and a budding entrepreneur like himself—would need going forward.

But Hoang wanted to learn more. So he acquired a Ph.D. from the University of Brussels, before becoming a serial entrepreneur. That time spent in Europe gave him another perspective from which to view Vietnam and the world, understanding more about how Europeans think and observe, which is a different slant from older Vietnamese who worked or studied in the former Soviet Union or younger Vietnamese who go to England or Australia, the U.S. or China.

During his serial entrepreneurial days, he too has started firms and failed and learned heaps in the process. For several years, now, he has been a successful consultant and researcher in Vietnam, becoming one of the most trusted advisors to business and government leaders, as well as communist party leaders. He sits on the Hanoi Stock Exchange's HNX-30 Index Committee, is a lecturer at several universities, and has started several advisory firms. Long an astute observer of economic issues in the country, Hoang won Vietnam's National Book award in 2007 and National Journalism award in 2010. Finally, Hoang exemplifies the bridge generation—he has faced many hardships as a child and adult, has watched the country change, and recognizes, perhaps more than many, some of the pitfalls and possible danger zones that it could encounter in the future unless it finds a clear pathway to succeed.

Nancy has been an outsider inching closer to understanding Vietnam and its people for nearly 20 years. When we met, she was an American professor, helping one of Vietnam's top universities—the National Economics University—establish the country's first international standard business school. The process was, in essence, a start-up venture, supporting development of the business school's infrastructure, financial and technology systems, product and service offerings through academic and corporate training programs and other activities. She spent nine years (1994-2003) involved in the $8.5 million capacity building project, delivering Boise State University's masters of business program to more than 80 Vietnamese professors, business and government experts. Not an easy task, yet through it all, she fell in love with the country and the people she worked with. She continues to teach and do research in Vietnam and in 2011 was awarded the Ministry of Education and Training's Medal of Honor, given to foreigners who have contributed to education in Vietnam.

Individually and together, we have watched and analyzed Vietnam's changes. When we first met, food rationing was still a recent memory when "gifted" children who performed well in school received "pecuniary rights" for their families, allowing more access to food and supplies. In the 1990s, the average city dweller rode a Chinese made bicycle. By 2010, most were able buy a Japanese motorbike. Today, in the larger cities, on a surface level at least, the economy has grown to a point where international brands proliferate—from Gucci and BMW to KFC and Starbucks. Foreigners may continue to be the bulk of the purchasers but the younger Vietnamese generations are in close pursuit, scooping up "copies" that get better every year.

*
* *

We have written the book in a style that we hope you find easy to read and understand. The chapters are relatively short, many use stories from our own and others' experience to make a point, and we include trigger questions at the end of many chapters to keep you thinking about the point and how it might help all of us better understand each other and ourselves. Throughout the book, we do include a few somewhat longer chapters or essays for reflection, again to bolster some of the points we are making and in a way that may be easier for some readers to access. Finally, at the end of the book, we have a Fact Sheet about Vietnam so readers can understand some of the basics of the country.

We've divided the book into three parts: What We See, Why We Worry, and Why We Hope. First, we talk about two big pieces of Vietnamese life that we see and that we think are having and will have major long term impacts. Those elements are simply the legacy of Vietnam's traditional cultural values and the shift to the market economy. Both have significant influence on the way people behave and think now and could do so in the future, even as both elements face some challenges.

Part II, Why We Worry, focuses on some of the implications of what we see, in terms of how what we call Vietnam's version of traditional Confucianism may affect some aspects of business life going forward. For example, the emphasis on strict hierarchy may, we fear, thwart some of the creativity and flow of ideas that Vietnam claims to desire. Further, the shift to a market economy appears to be not well understood by many, especially in terms of realizing the yin and yang of benefits *and* risk.

The third part, Why We Hope, points to our optimism for Vietnam and its people. At least three characteristics have emerged consistently within Vietnam over time and we see and hope they continue: the ability to be "resource-full" even in times of scarcity, the ability to be resilient under conditions of hardship or ambiguity, and the ability to reinvent oneself, and perhaps even a country, when necessary. Last, we put faith in the bridge generation, as well as current leaders who you will meet in this book. They are the visionaries, the Vietnamese evangelists who believe in, work hard for, and will help lead the country into its next 2,000 years.

But before we start, here's your first trigger question:

Think About It: For American readers: What assumptions do YOU have about Vietnam? List three. For Vietnamese readers: What assumptions do YOU have about your own country? How would you describe its three biggest strengths and its three biggest weaknesses?

1) _ Vietnamese dislike Americans

2) - Hanoi is older city that does not have the conv of developed Countries

3) _ Many Vietnamese are unethical & will try to steal from you

Part I

WHAT WE SEE

PART I: WHAT WE SEE

Let's start with some observations about Vietnam old and new. Compared to the U.S., Vietnam is indeed an old country. Its 2,000 years of recorded history (and 4,000 years in total, some say) humble most Americans, whose families arrived on the continent of North America 10 or 100 or at most 200 years before. Yet, Vietnam's capitol city, Hanoi, celebrated its 1000th birthday in 2010. Any Vietnamese trying to explain such time passage will also remind visitors that the Chinese invaded and stayed in Vietnam for 1000 years, that the French did the same for 100 and the Americans for 25 years. That history makes America's 250 years of history seem like it has just entered teenage-hood.

On the other hand, Vietnam is a young country in many ways. When visitors walk around the cities or villages, one of the most dramatic observations is that this population is not what you'd see in a place like Arizona or Japan. The Vietnamese themselves are young: over 60 % of Vietnam's 92 million people are under age 40 (and by the time you read this, the population numbers will already be out of date!). They have no or almost no memory of the American War, the Cambodian or Chinese Wars in the 1960s-1990s. The country is young politically and economically as well. It gained independence on Sept 2, 1945 but it took 30 more years before it unified in 1975. Another 20 years passed until the seeds of a market oriented economy began, and then another 10-15 years to work up steam.

Mr. Nguyên Trung Thanh has followed such changes in the country for years. He has been Vietnamese Ambassador to Singapore and a Fulbright Scholar, and currently is Ambassador and Permanent Resident Representative of the Vietnamese Diplomatic Mission in Geneva. As he says, during this recent period in history, the Vietnamese have "seen an open world to work with and learn from. This is unprecedented in Vietnamese history because for the most part, the country and people dealt with China and surrounding cultural societies. So now is the time for Vietnamese to learn about a global world." And, of course, the learning needs to go both ways—Vietnamese learning from foreigners and foreigners learning from Vietnamese as this old and young country moves forward.

Indeed, to quote the diplomat(ic) Mr. Thanh again, many in Vietnam have a "village mentality," struggling to join the broader world. Such a struggle comes partly, we think, from some very long standing traditions that may encounter new ones. In Vietnam's case, we see two striking elements that play big roles. First is the legacy of what we call the "Vietnamese version of Confucianism," or the traditional cultural values that are embedded in Vietnamese society. Second, we see the emergence of a market economy as key to understanding Vietnam and its future. In this next part of the book, we'll talk about some of those key cultural values and then we'll talk about some of the ways that the market economy is raising new questions and topics for Vietnam.

The Legacy of Traditional Vietnamese Cultural Values

Mr. Hoang Ngoc is a "journalist's journalist." Without being conscious of it, about every two minutes, he runs his fingers through his longish hair, pushing it out of his face. His mustache seems like an afterthought, a place to catch the odd ash from his cigarette as he stands and observes, slightly apart from the group. His eyes are like a crocodile's, half closed, but like a crocodile, he may look sleepy but he's catching more than most people. And he always has his camera nearby. He doesn't seem to be a person who would be intimidated or frightened of anything. But as a young soldier, he was both intimidated and frightened once, and he wasn't even on the battlefield.

Ngoc was in the Vietnamese army from 1985-1987. At the end of 1985, he received leave to go on holiday to Hanoi from his post on Vietnam's northern border with China. He had friends who had been scouts inside the Chinese territory and they offered to make some purchases for him that would be useful on the market at home. They brought him velvet cloth, which would become curtains, and—even more precious—so-called "peacock blankets," soft silk that could be made into women's undergarments and sold for a nice profit. He tucked them deep into his backpack and was ready to leave. But then, his supervisor asked Ngoc to do something for him.

The supervisor wanted Ngoc to transport a wooden bed frame and wardrobe back to Hanoi, despite strict regulations against such actions. But this was his boss and Ngoc could not refuse. So Ngoc found himself at Yen Bai railway station, talking to the military police. They asked where the wooden furniture came from, who was transporting it, why it was being shipped to Hanoi, and what Ngoc's role was. At any time, Ngoc could have been arrested, the furniture confiscated, and Ngoc's life would have changed course.

But at last, the police agreed to clear the bed frame and wardrobe. By then, Ngoc had missed his train and began to panic again. He still had the (illegal) Chinese cloth and blanket in his backpack. He slumped on a bench, fuming and scared and blaming his superior who had ordered him to transport the furniture and then left him alone at the station to take whatever trouble came.

The policemen noticed that Ngoc was still in the station, even though they had finished with him. They walked over as he tried to look invisible. No luck. So he told them that now he had missed the train because of his supervisor's demand. The policemen took pity on the young soldier and in the process, they explained some of life's harsh realities. Had it gone wrong, Ngoc's supervisor would never have acknowledged Ngoc or helped get him out of trouble. In fact, the policemen said, the supervisor probably had not even thought twice about putting the young soldier into such a situation, jeopardizing his safety or caring whether he went to jail. He was the supervisor and fully expected his underling to do what was asked. If Ngoc had been charged because he was transporting goods he was not supposed to, it would be his problem, not the supervisor's. Then the police helped Ngoc get the next train so he could continue home.

Ngoc's experience is an example of Vietnam's traditional cultural values in the raw. Someone further up in the hierarchy can ask someone lower down to do a task, illegal or not, easy or not. The subordinate is expected to do as told, and almost always follows through. No matter that such actions could put him at risk for jail and, at a minimum, disrupt plans. In a society based upon unequal relationships, especially vertical ones, Ngoc could not ask questions, could not challenge, and could not refuse. Key to this thinking is that in a culture like Vietnam's where hierarchy and the notion of unequal relationships is accepted, a current supervisor could influence the career path of his subordinate in the future, sometimes in the quite distant future. A stain on a resume could limit a promising career.

Easy for Vietnamese to understand. Many Americans would claim it never happens. But don't jump too fast.

Think About It: Recall a time when your supervisor or parents or an older sibling demanded you do something that could have caused you harm or gotten you into trouble. WHY did you do it?

*

*   *

Nguyên Pham Muoi, a *Wall Street Journal* journalist based in Vietnam, is knowledgeable, smart but also patient when it comes to his long-term vision for Vietnam's development. He sees a need for a "road map" for the future, understands the tensions of development but feels Vietnamese need to understand globalization, geopolitics, and English, as well as their own culture as factors influencing their futures. But his attitude is not so common among many Vietnamese.

Muoi recalled a discussion he had with a Vietnamese government official several years ago that illustrates the difficulty of seeing what we live with. Over tea, the two men discussed the ups and downs of the economic transition in Vietnam. At some point, journalist commented that to solve some of the country's problems required taking cultural factors into account and how that might affect behavior. His colleague, the government official, burst into laughter.

"You are kidding. What does culture have to do with economic problems?"

The journalist was, of course, thinking about culture in terms of how people learn to behave, almost without thinking. But the government official, like many Vietnamese at the time, was thinking of culture as "art." In the Vietnamese language, the words for "culture" ("*văn hóa*") and "performance arts" ("*nghệ thuật biểu diễn*") often appear together ("*văn hóa-nghệ thuật*"), rather than separately. But with the influx of western business ideas into Vietnamese universities, some students, business managers and even members of the government, had begun using some concepts that were unknown—or invisible—in Vietnam. As a result, concepts like "corporate culture," or "organizational culture" and even "organizational politics" are popping up.

So the government official finally came to realize that a country's culture involved more than learning to dance or paint. So how does Vietnamese culture, and its version of Confucianism, in particular, come into play in terms of how Vietnam may be changing today? First, we need to understand what it is.

*

* *

The rich eat meat, the poor eat vegetables.

Confucian proverb

Confucius (Kong Fu Zi, 孔夫子, 551-479 BC) was born in Shandong Province (China) at the end of a brutal warfare period in China. He has long been considered among the most influential intellectual masters in ancient China, and other East Asian cultures, including Japan, Korea, and Vietnam. Confucius came from a blueblood family and became a teacher and "gentry scholar." His lectures, in a collection called the "Five Classics," cover his observations about socio-political events in history and how societies changed during some of the bloodiest periods in Chinese history (i.e. the Spring-Autumn Warfare Period of 777-481 BC and the Warring States Period of 403-220 BC)[2].

The Confucianism we are going to talk about is the "Vietnamese version" of Confucianism that was first introduced to Vietnam as early as the first century BC.[3] This

---

[2] Quan Hoang Vuong and Tri Dung Tran (2009). "Cultural dimensions of the Vietnamese private entrepreneurship," *IUP Journal of Entrepreneurship Development*, VI(3/4), 54-78.

[3] Trân Ngoc Thêm (2001). *Tim hieu ve ban sac van hoa Viêt Nam.* Hô Chi Minh City Publisher

set of cultural values was cultivated, brought into the society and promoted by feudalist governments over time. It was then reflected through social norms, life teachings, and lectures by scholars. The Eastern Han Dynasty's official, Shi Xie ("士燮" or "士燮, 137-226), who served as the Administrator of the Jiaozhi command, now known as the North of Vietnam, was regarded as the first Confucianism scholar in Vietnam. We will talk about the Vietnamese version because most, if not all, Vietnamese distinguish their version from the Chinese origin. For instance, Chinese Confucianism does not look at traders with the same level of contempt as the Vietnamese do, who put them on the lowest social rank. In addition, Vietnamese Confucianism is often said to be more of a synthesis of Confucianism, Taoism (also Daoism), and Buddhism.[4]

Even so, many of Confucius's ideas were adapted by the Vietnamese and seem deceptively simple. In essence, he thought individuals and groups should follow codes of conduct, which also defined held positions and roles, many of which fell into a certain hierarchy. Scholars and farmers were above merchants, for example. Older people were higher than younger people. Men were higher than women.

While the notion of unequal relationships is fundamental, some elements could change that. For instance, if an educated and well-connected man could find opportunities to improve his social status, the King(s) would notice him, and thus allow him (and almost always it was a "him" not a "her") the chance to climb the political ladder. Why was this so important? In East Asian societies like Vietnam, politics is everything from being able to provide more for your family to gaining power within the ruling structure to developing a network of friends who could help you climb even further.

---

[4] Trân Van Giau (1988). *Triet hoc va Tu tuong*. Hô Chi Minh City Publisher.

So, with a higher political status, a "gentleman" could gain economic power and, consequently, have more "meat to eat." Thus, the desire for status, power and money tie together and rich and powerful gentlemen who reach such a status help each other and keep the circle going.

The basic ideas of relationships and connection are key to building power in Vietnam and become even more important when they lead to monetary benefits. So even in an emerging market economy, this scholar who lived 2,500 years ago continues to hold great sway. Nearly all Vietnamese thus take for granted that connections create power and power creates money.

So what does this mean in terms of how the values play out today? In the next sections, we'll consider several examples of the "unequal relationship" that appear in Vietnamese traditional cultural values.

*
*   *

The duck and the egg

Beware when the egg tries to be smarter than the duck.

Old Vietnamese saying

Many years ago, at dinner with a Vietnamese family Nancy had known for years, she sat next to the teenage daughter, who was 15. Nancy asked the young girl what her favorite courses were in high school.

"Biology. I love biology. I want to study that in university. But I will need to go to a different university than what my father thinks."

Two years later, Nancy sat next to the same young lady at another family dinner. At this dinner, the daughter wore very fashionable eye glasses and a sophisticated haircut. They talked again about what she was studying and what she would do in university. The young woman leaned toward Nancy, lowered her voice and said, "I want to go into fashion."

"But I cannot. My father won't let me. I will study economics."

And indeed, she has. Her father is proud to report that his daughter is one of the top graduates in the university. This young "egg" could not pull away from the "duck," her father.

Hoang had an even more dramatic experience when a young person—"egg"—tried to move away from the duck. A young man had asked Hoang for advice on what to study in college. They talked for hours about the young man's likes and dislikes, wishes and visions for his future and the choices available to him. Together, they concluded that he should study mathematical economics, in part because of its value for the future of the country but more personally because it would be useful for helping the young man find a job. Both men left the discussion satisfied at the time spent. But the egg then returned home and the ducks began to speak.

The next day, the young student-to-be returned to Hoang. He had abandoned the choice of mathematical economics because his parents disagreed with the choice and would not support him if he pursued it. Oddly, his parents never attended college, had no understanding of the major or what types of jobs it might open for their son. That lack of knowledge about disciplines was, for them, irrelevant and the young man's view (and that of his advisor, Hoang), held no sway with them. Without further discussion, they told him what to study. The duck decided what the egg would do.

*

*   *

The idea that individuals should be able to choose what to study, what profession to pursue, where to live and who to marry goes without question in many parts of the world, including America. That makes it perhaps harder for Americans to understand a pattern that seems so different. Instead of pursuing education and university degrees that their parents suggest, many children of American parents, for instance, have chosen to "follow their bliss," as mythology expert Joseph Campbell enticed the world to do. They postpone careers, in part because of the economic recession and the lack of employment, but also because they've not found that "bliss" job.

Some "eggs" choose fields where economic gain may be low, but chance for self-fulfillment is high. Many, like Nancy's sons, have picked professions that are far from what their own parental "ducks" did (academics, business). Instead, one "egg" pursued school psychology, working within schools to help children with developmental and social problems; the other has gone into theater and acting, definitely a high risk field. Yet both are good at what they do, have chosen the fields because they wanted to, and are doing so early in their professional lives. Rather than wait until they "retire" from some high paying job they may not wish to do but feel they must because of financial or status reasons, many young Americans are choosing their own, sometimes defiant, paths. Also, when those children are "off the payroll" as their parents might say, and no longer dependent upon their parents for financial support, most parents would agree that their time of influence has waned.

Not so in most Vietnamese families. As the young woman who wanted to study biology and then later fashion showed, parents still make many decisions for their children. As the young man who wished to pursue mathematical economics learned, his parents—who lacked hard knowledge about university or career paths—still controlled his destiny. Confucius's acknowledged and accepted "unequal relationship" demands that the "duck" direct and the "egg" follows. And, it has worked overtly for years in Vietnam. Perhaps, though, some version of it exists elsewhere as well.

Think About It: What do you accept from your "elders" without questioning it? What would you NOT accept? What is the basis for your decision or actions?

A precious gift

In 2010, an American *Viêt Kiêu* friend of Hoang's told him a curious story. *Viêt Kiêu* is a term used for Vietnamese who immigrate to another country and then return to Vietnam to work or invest. In this case, Hoang's friend was traveling the country to learn about his family's homeland which, for him growing up in another country, was rather new. This dramatic story is one that most American women will not believe or agree with but in fact may not be so uncommon as a way to perceive some women's roles in Vietnam.

The young man traveled to the southern part of Vietnam, into an agricultural region. There, he met a farmer. Vietnam is a highly agricultural country but certain regions do much better than others, because of location. Since weather conditions in the south are quite favorable for farming, farmers there don't have to work as hard as farmers do in the northern part of the country. As a result, goes the common legend, farmers in the south spend much of their time sitting around, talking and drinking during the day. If they get hungry, they simply walk to a nearby river or pond to catch and eat frogs or eels that are readily available. At least that's the tale that farmers in the north perhaps would tell!

When the *Viêt Kiêu* visitor showed up, he began a casual conversation with the farmer. Since the farmer had time to spare, he invited his new friend to drink with him. In Vietnam, many men believe that drinking brings them closer together and in this case, it seemed to do the trick. After hours of drinking, the two men became "close friends," talking as though they were long-lost buddies, telling each other the deepest secrets of their lives.

At one point during the long day, the farmer became a bit emotional. He said to his new best friend, "You are really a great man. You are willing to listen to my life story all day. I have never had such a kind friend. So today, we become brothers, brothers who sacrifice for each other."

The *Viêt Kiêu* was moved by the farmer's kind words and himself became a bit emotional. He waited to see what might come next. They sat in silence, as brothers do. They drank more, as brothers do. Finally, the farmer said, "I know I am poor like many other farmers in this village. But a poor man is not a man who has nothing to give to his close friend. And I have a precious gift for you, my dear young friend."

Hoang's friend was both surprised and curious. Then the farmer said, "The gift is my sixteen year old, very beautiful daughter, to whom I have given the best love all my life."

*

*   *

In much of the world outside of the U.S., March 8 is International Women's Day. When Nancy and other foreign women visit Vietnam on the day, it sometimes seems odd. Men buy exorbitantly expensive—on that day—flowers for the women in their lives, from wives and mothers to colleagues and administrative assistants. Then they take their assistants to lunch. The men get drunk, the women listen to jokes, talk among themselves, and seem to enjoy the day. American women ask "why just one day?" But, of course, a visitor quickly realizes that on most other days, women get little overt appreciation, so perhaps at least one day is a good thing. Then again, with changes in the economy, might that change? What would Confucius say?

Women have very specific roles in Vietnam and mostly those come from our gentleman scholar of old. Confucius made clear that women are critical to the smooth workings of society and their roles show the importance for that. They educate children, keep the home, and manage the family's money. Sounds powerful, but it was still an unequal relationship in terms of roles.

In Confucius's day, a scholar was depicted as naïve student, who spent his time focusing on understanding Confucian teachings, thus leaving the matters of daily life to his woman (and not uncommonly, his women). Thus, women gave the student-husbands a home, food, sex and most importantly, books so they could continue studying and learning. But, as with so many other unequal relationships, Vietnamese cultural values hold that a woman must support her man unconditionally. This resulted, of course, in a married woman suppressing her own desires and aspirations, especially to acquire education, to support a husband in his.

Women are an increasingly important part of Vietnam's workforce, representing half of the country's workforce. So, with some of the changes that are coming, we have to wonder if traditional roles will still dominate going forward in Vietnamese society.

So what's changing? More Vietnamese women marry foreigners,[5] despite reports of ill treatment, even murders of young Vietnamese wives, in countries ranging from South Korea and Taiwan to China.[6] Also, more educated Vietnamese women are marrying educated Vietnamese men, often men who have studied or worked abroad and seen other ways that men and women interact. The women themselves may have studied or traveled abroad and seen what women in other countries expect and do. As they bring back those ideas for themselves and their daughters (and, we hope, sons), could there be signs of roles shifting?

Think About It: *Some in the U.S. may think women's roles are far advanced. Yet recent years of legislation and conflict over issues from workplace discrimination to the right to choose raise a question of just how much control women do have over their own positions. Likewise, in Vietnam, what holds women to their traditional roles as they begin to see alternative ways of operating?*

*

*   *

---

[5] AFP (2010). "Vietnamese brides flock to South Korea," *The Independent*, Aug. 8. <http://www.independent.co.uk/life-style/vietnamese-brides-flock-to-south-korea-2047193.html>

[6] Jason Lim (2010). "Murder of Vietnamese Wife," *The Korean Times*, Jul. 19.<http://www.koreatimes.co.kr/www/news/opinon/2013/01/352_69748.html>

Traditional social values at work

The department head sat opposite a foreigner at a large conference table just in front of his desk. The desk, table and chairs took up most of the office space, so that the musty room felt especially cozy even though the air conditioner blew hard enough for the gauze curtains to move. A secretary placed a soft knock on the door and then opened the door and walked in just as the department head was telling her to enter.

Mrs. Anh opened the door, leaning sideways as she looked around the door into the office. She walked in, placed a few papers on the edge of the conference table in front of the department head, mentioned that he needed to sign the papers, then turned and walked out.

"That is very bad, very bad. Her behavior is disrespectful," said the manager as he shook his head.

"She came into the office without waiting for me to tell her. She put these papers on the desk, did not hand them to me." He gestured how she should have held the papers with two hands so they were facing him, and offered them to him while bending in a small bow.

"And then she turned her back to me as she left the room. Very impolite."

Here was a man in his early 40s, complaining about a woman in her early 30s who was labeled "impolite"; HE was the boss, HE was the male, HE was educated, HE was older. And she disrespected him—by not waiting for a command to enter, by putting papers on a desk and not in his two hands, and by walking out of the room face forward: the "master-follower," unequal relationship at work.

But is that just Vietnamese cultural values at work or do such attitudes exist elsewhere?

Think About It: How do you behave with colleagues, especially subordinates at work? Are they expected to show deference? How? Why?

*

*   *

Within 10 minutes after arriving at work one morning, Nancy held three bouquets of flowers.

"Happy Teacher's Day!"

While the U.S. may have National Teacher Appreciation Week, it pales in comparison to November 20 in Vietnam. University professors take flowers to their favorite kindergarten teachers, junior high and high school teachers, and their own university professors. Then they rush home to await visits from their own students.

Partly because of the early attention and respect that Confucius demanded as a scholar and for other scholars, they hold top positions in the status ladder. As a result, an aloofness surrounds "Professors" or elders, which comes with expectations that underlings will be at their beck and call. The attitude is resolute, unquestioned, and gives off the odor of sovereignty of a feudal lord.

But the relationship goes both ways.

*

*   *

The Vietnamese—and other Asians—see their teachers as guardians of their futures, as confidants when they need them, and often, as solvers of their problems. In many ways the power that teachers hold over current and former students is overwhelming and uncomfortable; on the other hand, students hold enormous power as well.

"Teacher, can you help me?"

Mr. G. was in masters program that Nancy managed. In his late thirties, he had a round face and glasses fixed tightly to his nose bridge. He stood in the "I'm being respectful to my teacher" pose, arms folded in front of him loosely, shoulders hunched forward, and looking toward the ground with short upward glances.

He was struggling in the program. His grades were low; his written work was clearly his own, because the grammar and spelling were so poor. While many participants masked their incomprehension in class simply by nodding, Mr. G. sat with a cocked head, questions in his eyes but unable to get them out.

Yet he was a gentle man, and his integrity seemed solid. His superiors asked that he be allowed into the program, despite his low entrance requirement qualifications. His math skills seemed strong, but the rest of his work was not. Perhaps his poor English was the root cause, but there was little time or way to find out.

"I must complete this course. I cannot fail. Can you please help me?"

Imploring a teacher, nearly begging for assistance, fits the pattern of honoring the teacher.

"She has the power to make it right for me and help me save face. She can allow me to finish and get this degree so my family will be proud," he was probably thinking.

But "international academic standards" were at issue, ones that all participants had to meet to complete a degree program. Unfortunately, time had run out for him. Mr. G. was no longer on probation and needed to leave the program.

A case like this would be clear in the U.S. but is gray in Vietnam, in part because of the unequal relationship between student and teacher. While a teacher can make excessive demands on their students, part of the bargain is that teachers will take care of and look out for their students, for their whole lives. Benevolence, a key idea for Vietnamese culture, goes both ways.

And that's where The Professor and The Student were on that muggy afternoon.

"You are my teacher. You are my big sister. You can help me."

It's hard for non-Vietnamese to realize what a compliment and what an obligation those words are.

It was a long afternoon on the red plastic couch in the hallway of the university.

Think About It: *What obligations—spoken and not—do you face in your work life? Why do they exist and how do you respond to them? Why?*

Respect Kurt & Jack
Can disagree but always be respectful

The closed world of trust

The theory of "six degrees of separation" is common party game material in the U.S. The game involves asking how many steps or contacts would it take to gain access to some famous person, like the U.S. President or Bill Gates or Angelina Jolie? (Nancy calculates two, three and five for herself. Lesson: is it easier to reach the president than a movie star?). In Vietnam, Hoang's equivalent degrees of separation would likely never exceed two—to reach

Vietnam's Prime Minister or President, top business leaders, or even movie stars.

In Vietnam, relationships and finding ways to connect with people is more than a game. It's a way of getting things done, from helping a child get into college or find a job, to gaining a business contract or attaining a government position. Having a network and access in Vietnam is undeniably required and if you are outside the circles that count, you are invisible. While many Vietnamese would say they could never "reach the prime minister" through their connections, all enjoy explaining the intricate web of personal relationships—that a friend is the nephew of a famous military leader or the daughter-in-law of a former foreign minister.

Relationships also matter, of course, when it comes to information and, like most people, Vietnamese thrive on the type that comes informally. Some Vietnamese would argue that the best way to understand the Vietnamese is to visit a *Bia Hoi,* one of the open air beer restaurants that dot street corners in every town, large or small. As economist Vo Tri Thanh once said to a Japanese visitor, "*Bia Hoi* is the *Vietnamese internet.* You can find everything you want to hear there." Information is "stored on (the equivalent of) sophisticated electronic servers" at separate tables where different groups drink and overhear what's happening at the next table.

But for most foreigners, even some who speak Vietnamese, the circles of connection in Vietnam are often closed. That said, it is possible to move closer to the inside of various circles, but it takes time and incredible patience.

After working closely with university colleagues for six years, Nancy sat in a conference room one afternoon at the end of the work day about to face an uncomfortable discussion. Surrounded by a dozen Vietnamese colleagues, all but one who was also extremely uncomfortable, she faced down a manager who was livid about a decision she and her project partner had made. As he railed on, Nancy sat without moving, saying nothing during the 20 minute tirade. Then it was her turn to explain the decision's rationale, the implications, and the input that Vietnamese colleagues around the table (but remaining unnamed) had offered before the final decision was made. But the manager wasn't buying it and the meeting ended on a tense note.

The next day, the most senior colleague at the meeting stopped by to say she was surprised that Nancy had stayed calm and "saved face," even as her colleague was so upset, and showed his anger. But then, she mentioned almost in passing, he must feel more comfortable and have more trust because otherwise, he would never have shown such a temper. Implication: Nancy had moved one small step on the concentric circles closer to the inside, even as an outsider.

*

*   *

So what do incidents like this mean? First, unequal relationships—between insiders and outsiders—will always continue, even though they may shift somewhat over time. The second idea stems from the first and it deals with how people think of trust.

In a very general sense, Vietnamese and Americans come from different perspectives when it comes to trust. Many Americans start with an assumption of trust at the beginning of a relationship. It can be lost, to be sure, but many assume that it's fundamental to a relationship that is growing and is reciprocal unless proven otherwise.

Vietnamese, in contrast, generally start with a premise that trust must be earned over time, usually a long time.

Once again, the notion of unequal relationships reigns. With people who are not from the same village or school or university, their initial stance is wariness and distrust, rather than openness and trust. It makes sense, of course, because of the Vietnamese history of betrayal by neighbors and other countries from far away. But beyond that, the deep cultural values around hierarchy and focus on family and nearby neighbors sets up the expectation that one can trust only those on the inside.

It explains, too, an early (1990s) attitude of Vietnamese when electronic mail began to appear. For many international users, e-introductions are a matter of course. Nancy receives emails from colleagues all over the world introducing her to others and she does the same—making cross-border virtual introductions. These newly introduced colleagues correspond, exchange ideas and help each other largely because of the trust they have in the introducer. Not so with many Vietnamese. They were uncomfortable "talking" with or building a relationship with someone they had not met, face to face. As one Vietnamese colleague said "our unwillingness to trust through email may harm our ability to work with the rest of the world."

Most Vietnamese have moved past that strict stance but introductions, especially face to face, continue to be the preferred way to start a relationship. Only then, only after years sometimes, does trust begin to settle.

Dr. Nguyên Si Dung of the Vietnamese National Assembly (i.e. parliament) agrees with us that in general, Vietnamese highly regard relationships. Building close and trustworthy relationships is thus extremely important for doing business and for making contact with the Vietnamese community, including both businesspeople and policymakers.

He even went on with an observation that could be interesting to outsiders (who traditionally observe the business world's rule of "arm's length transaction"): "Sometimes Vietnamese sign a commercial contract with each other just to start establishing a new relationship." No wonder so many misunderstandings in negotiations may occur.

Think About It: Is our assumption correct? Do Americans build trust—or assume trust—when they first meet? Why would that be? Why would the opposite be true for Vietnamese?

Yes, to some extent but I do think there is an element of ... trust must be learned

Changes in the making?

Despite its strength, we see cracks in the legacy of traditional cultural values in Vietnam, both in terms of what some people think makes sense for them and in terms of changes in the economy. In part, the changes are due to the market economy changes, which we'll briefly review. Then, we'll show how a few individuals have begun to push against tradition and the role of money, short-term thinking, and choice.

Time out: A quick review of *Doi Moi* and the stages of renovation.

The Vietnamese economy has been moving toward a market economy for almost a quarter of a century, beginning with the Sixth National Congress of the Communist Party of

Vietnam in 1986. Changes have affected the thinking and mentality of most people in the country. So what's happened in the up-and-down ride of the last 25 years? We see at least four stages.

The period of "Entrepreneurial Policy-makers" (1987-1994): Early on, hyperinflation (think: 700%) took hold as the country introduced new institutions and new concepts, designed to encourage new firms and shifts toward market economics. By 1994, per capita GDP was $230/year, growth was rapid—averaging 8.5% yearly, and over 17,400 entrepreneurial firms started up.[7]

Trade and diplomatic normalization (1995-1999): As Vietnam and the U.S. began formal relations, trade and investment dramatically increased, from many sectors. Over $25 billion of FDI entered the country, billions of aid dollars flowed in from such institutions as the World Bank and Asian Development Bank. But the Asian financial turmoil hurt Vietnam and output growth declined to 4.8% by 1998. Afterward, the scheme for privatizing state-owned enterprises started in earnest and GDP per capita rose to $300 per year.

Boom times (2000-2006): On July 20, 2000, Vietnam's first stock market opened as the Hô Chi Minh City Stock Trade Center (HOSTC), later renamed the Hô Chi Minh City Stock Exchange (HOSE or HSX) on August 8, 2007. The exchange listed two firms when it opened and had 108 by the end of 2006. More striking, Vietnam's State Securities Commission reported that the number of trading accounts jumped from 2,908 (in 2000) to 120,000 (in 2006). At the end of 2006, the total capitalization of all firms listed on

---

[7] Quan Hoang Vuong (2010). *Financial markets in Vietnam's transition economy: Facts, insights, implication.* Saarbrücken, Germany: VDM Verlag.

Vietnam stock market reached 22.7% of the total GDP.[8] During this time, private enterprises mushroomed, turning into powerhouses like Saigon Securities Incorporation (financial services), FPT (information technology), Trung Nguyên (consumer goods), Techcombank (banking services), and many others. The average growth of 7.5% looked like Vietnam was another little tiger on the move.

Now what? (2007-present): The little tiger has not roared, as the pace of growth fell to about 5% in 2013, from a peak of 8.5% (2007). While GDP per capita is $1,600/year (maximum), the world is changing Vietnam's economy. The country's government and business leaders, as well as ordinary workers, have learned hard, expensive, and painful lessons about market mechanisms. Many state-run conglomerates, once the 'iron blows' of the market/socialist-oriented economy, now have huge losses and debt burdens. On 6 March 2008, Deputy Prime Minister Nguyên Sinh Hung, former Finance Minister and now Chairman of the National Assembly, stated that the stock market hit bottom when VNIndex was 611. Unfortunately, he was wrong. After a two-week recovery, VNIndex went down to less than 250 in February 2009. Since then, VNIndex has never reached 600. In 2013, there are about 500,000 enterprises in Vietnam and the country expects its annual output to reach $145 billion.

Increasingly, concern about misallocation of resources along with "crony capitalists and quasi-entrepreneurs" fill the newspapers and conversations. A typical example is tycoon Nguyên Duc Kiên, a senior commercial banker, who manipulated the banking industry and gold market before

---

[8] DHVP Research (2012). "Vietnam Celebrated Stock Markets' 12th Birthday," *Vietnamica.net*, Jul. 29. <http://www.vietnamica.net/vietnam-celebrated-stock-markets-12th-birthday/>

being arrested in August 2012. His arrest sent a chill through the Vietnamese stock markets for three consecutive days, during which most stocks lost 20% of their value.

A Vietnamese proverb says that a person experiences four periods in life—birth, old age, sickness, and death (*Sinh—Lao—Bênh—Tu*), before a rebirth. Is that Vietnam's next stage? In the meantime, we see challenges to the traditional cultural values: could that be part of the rebirthing process?

When the wrong answer is the right answer

In high school, Nghiêm Phu Kiên Cuong was good at chemistry. One day, the head chemistry teacher assigned the students a task to write about their personal methods of learning. Interesting question in itself, since much of the schooling in Vietnam was (and still is) more rote "chalk and talk," where the teacher writes information on a chalk board, and the students copy and memorize it. No questions, no discussion. A one way flow of information and an assumption that it will stick. For the most part, because students are quite good at rote memorizing, the information does stay in their heads, at least until exams come. A bigger question, which we will talk about more later, is whether students can deal with unstructured problems: can they think, analyze, and solve problems that aren't easy to describe and answer from information written on a board.

Cuong found the teacher's assignment challenging. He took it to heart and tried to analyze his approach to learning. Unfortunately, the answer that came out of his analysis and the process he used got him into trouble.

He struggled for a day or two, and finally wrote a three-line summary of his approach to learning:

1. Listen carefully and attentively to the subject teacher during class hours.
2. Do the textbook exercises after re-reading pieces of theory.
3. Notice circumstances where a particular problem-solving skill is particularly useful.

Alas, it was not the right answer.

His teacher wanted a "longer report, well-written and great-looking," and Cuong's was far from that mark. When he talked with his teacher, Cuong argued that his response reflected the simplicity of his learning method. He refused to change what he had submitted. His teacher became furious at Cuong's impertinence, asked Cuong to borrow a "nicely written report" from a classmate and follow suit, to make his own more acceptable. Again, Cuong declined to change his report. The teacher expelled Cuong from class for a week and asked for a meeting with Cuong's father.

In the Vietnamese society, a scholar or teacher is the highest rung of society. The respect appears in many ways, including Teacher's Day, set aside to honor teachers. A teacher is always revered, no matter what the former students' ages. Even when they become successful business managers, politicians, or educators themselves, they defer to former teachers. If a teacher asks a current or former student to complete a task, or take action on some request, it happens. The hierarchy never wavers. So for Cuong to confront and refuse a request from his teacher was tantamount to striking him.

But also, the relationship of a father to son is sacred as well. Cuong, like most young Vietnamese men, admired his father, saw him as a teacher of the family, and never wanted to let him down. As a grown man today, he still says that his father, who died a decade ago, was the greatest influence in his life. So, naturally, the high school student Cuong was nervous about the meeting between his father and his teacher. He dreaded his father's return.

But after the meeting, his father did not reprimand Cuong or say anything about what had happened during the meeting with the teacher. As Cuong recalls it, his father spoke softly and said, "It was not your fault. You did the right thing."

In Vietnamese society, not everyone has or feels he can follow his own beliefs. When people lived on farms and small villages, they needed to support each other and keep the village safe. To act independently could harm the bigger group. As a result, the meaning of "right" and "wrong" became more about being accepted by the group, not your own beliefs or desires.

Yet as a young man, Cuong challenged tradition and fought back.

Think About It: When did you confront a demand and refuse to do it? Why?

*

*   *

Money as king?

When times were tough, education mattered less. Parents wanted daughters to marry men who made money and could feed them, not impoverished scholars who studied. As many said, "you can't eat an education." Until the market economy began to take hold, in the mid1990s, the best jobs were ones that brought people closer to food supplies or that generated petty cash. So the best jobs were vehicle drivers and food sellers, even if most of the food was low quality and sold in state-run shops, at subsidized prices.

But that may be changing. Today, education means money, and money means status.

In a graduate business class in one of Hanoi's top universities, a visiting American professor stood before 40 eager Vietnamese students, sitting at rows of desks, four to a desk. The group ranged in age from about 22 to 30. Some had several years of experience with foreign firms as assistant managers; others came directly from undergraduate programs in business or economics and had never worked. Their English language skills could be deceptively good—or poor: some students can carry on discussions about economics and business at a level common in much of the world, and then when the discussion goes into specifics, they flounder; others stare straight ahead, nod knowingly, but then show no emotion to a joke, a key comment, or a question because they've no idea what the discussion is about.

But they have one thing in common.

They want to be rich. These young Vietnamese arrive on motorbikes—or in the odd cars with drivers. They wear name brand clothes (or copies): Tommy Hilfiger and Lacoste shirts, Pierre Cardin belts, Prada and Coach bags and Nike sneakers. They may carry Nokia mobile phones but they often say they want iPhones or the Samsung Galaxy S3. Indeed, Mrs. Pham Chi Lan, retired economist for the Vietnam Chamber of Commerce, has noted that some 50% of Vietnamese students say they want to "make money first, then they will do good things for their community."

When their professor asks what they want to be in their future lives, they don't respond by saying "an IT manager" or "a banker" or "I want to start a company." No, their responses are "I want to be a millionaire. I want to be like Bill Gates," whose appearance in town rivals or surpasses the excitement of any political figure. But although the young students may be an aspiring Bill Gates or Warren Buffet, some Vietnamese are already there. And they too are fast becoming celebrities.

Is money now "king" in Vietnam?

*

*   *

On March 5, 2013, major business newspapers throughout Vietnam reported that Pham Nhât Vuong, the owner of Vingroup, Vietnam's largest real estate business, joined *Forbes's* list of the world's wealthiest people. Ranked number 974, *Forbes* estimated Vuong's personal wealth, consisting mainly of Vingroup's shares listed on the Hô Chi Minh City Stock Exchange (HSX), to be worth US$1.5 billion. For the first time in Vietnam's 2000+ year history, a billionaire joined the ranks of the world's high-profile rich.[9] But just what did Vuong's "accomplishment" mean for the ordinary Vietnamese? When Vuong joined the *Forbes* list, DHVP Research, an economic advisory firm in Hanoi, surveyed 150 Vietnamese for their views about Vuong becoming one of the top 1000 richest people in the world. Granted, the opinions came from internet users and mostly younger Vietnamese but nonetheless, their views diverged widely.

Many people questioned how Vuong was able to amass such wealth in what is still a very poor country. His wealth

---

[9] Forbes, March 5, 2013. <http://www.forbes.com/profile/pham-nhat-vuong/>

comes largely from land and residential housing values that rose quickly before the land and housing bubble burst. As a result, some people questioned whether he truly did have as much wealth as *Forbes* estimated or if it had dropped because of the financial crisis.

Other people commented that the bubble burst caused the bulk of Vietnam's economic troubles, which was the most severe since the launch of market renovation in 1986. Could Vuong, instead of being a hero, have contributed to the difficult economic woes that the country now faces? Still others who were polled said they really did not care about Vuong, as an individual or wealthy icon. Rather, they feared for their own finances and found his celebrity too much to bear. How could he be in such a situation while they were still struggling to make a life? In contrast, some people found Vuong's new title to be inspirational, a sort of "spiritual encouragement" and guiding light for the notion of entrepreneurship and future entrepreneurs. If this man, like so many Vietnamese from humble beginnings, could reach a pinnacle of public and international "success," certainly others could do the same. Finally, some people felt that Vuong's ranking gave them and the whole country something to be proud of as a symbol of Vietnam's rising economic prosperity.[10]

Vuong is not the only man in Vietnam famous for generating a fortune. A few months before *Forbes* profiled Vuong's achievement, the magazine highlighted yet another Vietnamese entrepreneur. In late July 2012, *Forbes* published an article about Dang Lê Nguyên Vu, who owns Vietnam's best-known private coffee brand, Trung Nguyên. *Forbes* reporter Scott Harris estimated Vu's net worth at $100

---

[10] Vietfin.net, March 6, 2013. <http://www.vietfin.net/khao-sat-y-kien-xa-hoi-ve-su-kien-ty-phu-dola-dau-tien-pham-nhat-vuong/>

million, "a mind-boggling sum in a country whose per capita income is $1,300."[11]

Vu is an entrepreneur who takes risks. He left medical school to return to the central highlands where he grew up and began working in the coffee fields. Eventually, he built the Trung Nguyên brand into a major coffee producer, set up over 1000 coffee cafes around the country, and has begun to push the idea of "responsible creativity" and "the coffee spirit," which we'll return to in the section about why we are hopeful about Vietnam.

People like Vuong and Vu offer a paradox for the Vietnamese. The young people see and read about the wealth that these men are (now) known for. They want, as the young graduate students said, "to be millionaires," as if that is something that one can buy off a shelf in a retail store. Some miss the point that these two Vietnamese grown and bred entrepreneurs, like true entrepreneurs anywhere, spent years before they had any real money, that they worked hard because they loved their fields and wanted to build a business, not to make money. That came later.

So Vietnam faces a period of learning that "money = hard work" first, and the "being rich" part comes later, if at all.

Think About It: *How can young people learn that making money is harder than it looks or that an "overnight success" can take a decade to reach!? We may think that Vietnamese young people are unique in this thinking, but does it happen in America as well?*

---

[11] Forbes, July 25, 2013. <http://www.forbes.com/sites/forbesasia/2012/07/25/vietnams-coffee-king-dang-le-nguyen-vu/>

*
*   *

Learning the hard way that market economics has risks

One of Hoang's old friends, Cuong (who challenged his high school chemistry teacher), found a job at Việt-Duc Hospital (Hanoi) as an accountant, on the cusp of the market economy changes. He and his wife, like so many eager Vietnamese at the dawn of the market economy, wanted to build a house. In Vietnam, where relationships matter in so many aspects of life, Cuong had a relative who wanted to help him with his house project. In particular, the relative wanted to help Cuong financially and offered to introduce Cuong to a banker he knew. The banker then helped Cuong borrow VND 300 million in 2007. (VND is currency symbol for the local currency, Vietnamese Dong; at the time of the story, VND 300 million was equivalent to about US$20,000). Since Cuong needed only VND 150 million for the construction of a house, Cuong followed his relative's advice and became what many at the time was called a "nano-scaled capitalist."

Cuong lent half of his loan funding to a third party borrower at double the interest rate he was paying to the banker. Had the scheme worked, the third-party borrower would finance the cost of funds for Cuong's house. And this is where Cuong learned that the market economy—and real estate in particular—has risks, as well as gains. The borrower went bankrupt and disappeared, leaving Cuong with the full debt burden. A hard lesson and bitter experience about market transactions: the danger of making such a decision himself, on the advice from what he assumed were reliable (and knowledgeable) people, and being duped by an uncreditworthy borrower.

After his experience, Cuong became more sensitive to the importance, and difficulty, of gaining financial independence. Like many Vietnamese, he believed that the economy, which appeared stable in the 1998-2005 period, would continue to expand. Faced with tough blows of the real-world financial transactions, he realized that the market economy does not always improve and make participants wealthy. The upsides were so tempting that most people, including Cuong, didn't think about the potential downsides. To pay off the debt and cover the loss of bank-loaned money, Cuong used his own funds, which accounted for just a fraction of the obligation, and had to ask for support from his mother and his uncle's wife. He repaid the debts, finally earned back enough money to build a house, and learned a lesson about market economics the hard way.

If you find Cuong's story puzzling (his naiveté, his too simple understanding about the notion of risk), Dr. Nguyên Si Dung, of the Vietnamese National Assembly, may have a telling insight:

> Vietnamese are receptive to new things and ideas and can be very fast learners. But few really understand them deeply. This has an important implication. If a foreign businessperson wants to have a successful business with Vietnamese, she should do everything to make sure that her Vietnamese partner really spends time and effort to study and genuinely master the new business concept, product technology and management process.

The wisdom of housewives

When Nancy lived in Vietnam, she had a wonderful cook and housekeeper who took care of her. And without knowing it, Mrs. Ha understood market economics.

When Nancy asked for tomatoes in a salad in April, or mangos in November, Ha said, "No tomatoes. No mangos."

"Not the season. Tomatoes are in the south and not the north today. No tomatoes."

Mrs. Ha bought fruits and vegetables only when they were available locally—and at a reasonable price. So weeks and months would pass without certain food, until they became available once again. Of course, the locally sourced tomatoes and mangos were far more tasty than the ones Nancy got in the U.S. that were shipped from Mexico or Peru, arrived hard as rocks and never quite ripened the same way.

Mrs. Ha and most Vietnamese housewives have understood and used the market economy for years, even during the decades of the planned economy. They go to the wet market to buy fish and chickens and, as part of the process, they bargain. There was (and is) no "set price," there was no "planned economy price," there was simply the price that the fish mongers could command that day at that market with that housewife. The housewife inherently knew risk—if she chose badly and bought a fish that was spoiled or for a price that was may be too high, it was her fault. But when she found a particularly good fish and bargained the seller down to a price lower than she expected, it was the housewife's gain.

Market economics, pure and simple. Interesting that the concepts of risk and gain are so clear in the wet market, and so murky elsewhere. Or are they?

Think About It: *Where have you experienced real market economics at work? Even though many people think the U.S. is a market economy, try to consider any situation where there are no regulations or no pricing structure to get in the way.*

*

*   *

Upside down market economics

Just when you think you understand how an economic system is changing—poof—it doesn't work the way it's supposed to. Take vehicles in Hanoi as an example.

To many foreigners, motorbikes symbolize Vietnam's progress and a thriving economic system. Indeed, the dramatic changes in vehicle mix on the roads of large cities are most obvious when it comes to motorbikes, especially those under 125cc. But first, a trip back in memory: in the early 1990s, Hanoi's vehicle mix was lopsided—Chinese made bicycles dominated the streets, with about 85-90% of vehicles. The Honda Dream II motorbikes on the road were few and coveted. Russian-made smoke-belching trucks and spiffy white Toyota Land Cruisers were the only four-wheeled vehicles, plus a few used sedans. Traffic moved at the pace of bikes, but the few motorbikes made known their presence with horns that sounded like trucks.

Fast forward 15 years.

Bicycles have nearly disappeared, cars are frequent and pesky, but motorbikes now dominate the streets. The rise in motorbikes offers a visible contrast to Vietnam's poverty, to be sure, but also links to what's happened with the ability to be more productive as a country. At the end of 1980s and into the 1990s, most Vietnamese adults used bikes as their main means of transportation, but the bikes were heavy and slow. To bike faster, then, required people to use more calories, which was a hardship since most could afford only half of a kilo of meat per month, which meant their available daily calories were limited. Also, slow bikes meant it took longer to go anywhere and because the weather in Vietnam is often unpredictable and unpleasant, it meant people were in bad conditions for longer periods of time—in rainstorms and floods, heat and humidity, traffic pollution and potholes. It was not uncommon, during floods, to see people biking through water that topped the bike wheels, meaning their knees pushed up through the water with each pedal movement.

Spending so much time in the outside elements meant more chances to become—and stay—ill. More motorbikes means people reach their destinations more quickly, that they can carry more people (whole families of four or five are not uncommon), and that a family has the financial ability to purchase a bike, which can cost up to $2,000. Thus, motorbikes have become a symbol of economic growth and perhaps even better health. Nowadays, even a high-school student may receive a motorbike from her parents to save time and energy.

With motorbikes a boon to the economy, to energy, and to a healthier Vietnam, what could be the downsides? Some argue that motorbikes may represent the upside down thinking in a market economy—they may seem to bring prosperity but they also bring problems.

Motorbikes affect the economy in many ways, but two are particularly critical: in contributing to which parts of the cities may thrive or not and in changing the environment—both physical and perhaps mental.

*

* *

Some days in Hanoi, you can't help but think about the stories of London's fog in the close of the 1800s. The air is so thick with smoke that when people blow their noses or cough into handkerchiefs, they bring up black bile. Smoke from coal used for cooking, but even more so, pollution from vehicles has become a problem that increasingly worries parents. You have to wonder what Hanoi's residents' lungs look like.

On top of the air pollution, noise wears people down. Years ago, Nancy woke up one night in her house on Triêu Viêt Vuong about 2:00 AM. The street was narrow, filled with houses and a few storefronts, a real neighborhood towards the southern part of Hanoi. But her neighbor across the street decided that the middle of the night was a good time to work on his motorbike and as though he was in a bubble, he did just that. No one said a thing, since it happened all the time. But that noise was nothing compared to the daily blaring of horns—from motorbikes, trucks, cars—that fills every street in the city. And interestingly, some Vietnamese claim that noise pollution may be worse than air pollution.

People get sick, not because of a tiring workday, but because of the noise they suffer two to three hours a day while commuting. Because motorbikes greatly outnumber cars, and because it sometimes seems that Vietnamese motorbike drivers are vying for the award of being the least patient drivers in the world, they use horns to take out their frustration and lack of patience. Sadly, some of them go further. Increasingly, there are cases of motorbike rage— motorbike drivers who hurt and even kill others because of their psychological instability while on the road.

Think About It: *Tradeoffs—what are you willing to give up for progress?*

The new world of choice

The most important period in the early part of my life as a person who was beginning to learn to think was 1983.

Dâu Thuy Ha
Consultant and business owner OCD

American readers, please try to imagine living in a world where you wear the same color and style of clothes that everyone else does, where you live in assigned housing, where food and other products are limited and everyone eats rice, noodles, and spinach leaves (or whatever the equivalent American food would be—perhaps hamburger meat, potatoes and tomatoes, day after day, for every meal). You have no option to choose where your children go to school, which hospital you visit, or what job you take. All of the shops sell the same types of pots or ladders or spices. Almost no choice.

That's the world Vietnamese who are 60 years old and older lived in for much of their early lives. Mrs. Pham Chi Lan, former Vietnam Chamber of Commerce economist, agrees.

Of course, from an American perspective, if you don't learn how to choose early in life, starting with which t-shirt to wear as a child, then how can you choose a career, a spouse, a car or a university when those options finally appear? As Ms. Lan says, even younger people at universities in Vietnam struggle with what major to choose, what path to take and how to balance their new opportunities with the desires of their family and worries about taking a different course.

*

*   *

Dâu Thuy Ha was designated as "a gifted student," when she was a child. This was not just a nice honor but an economic boon for her family. Gifted children helped their families secure "pecuniary rights," which meant they received more food and other supplies than did families where the children were not so designated. Ha continued to excel when she finished high school by receiving a coveted scholarship to study outside of Vietnam. In her case, she would study in Russia, in Moscow, no less, which was the motherland of communism and a sort of mentor for Vietnam. Her dream was to study Portuguese and do it in Moscow. Ha was on the road to a brilliant and exciting future.

Studying abroad was an honor, an adventure, but it also meant even more pressure. Any Vietnamese lucky enough to study in Russia or any East European country, which were of course the only options to study abroad, was seen as her family's savior, expected to "send substantial assets" back home. Ha fast found out what sending substantial assets home required and she learned about economic motivations in a way that might have made Karl Marx blush.

Ha looked forward to four years in a university and to follow her plan of learning Portuguese. But soon after arriving in Moscow, she had a lesson in the planned economy, Russian style. She received notice that she would be transferred to another university. Watch out exciting future, here comes Mother Russia in the form of new orders.

Forget Moscow, you're going to Simferopol, the capital of Crimea, 1,800 miles away in a remote province in Ukraine.

Forget Portuguese, you'll study Russian.

Ha was told, not asked. No choice, just do it.

As a cog in a central planning mechanism that sorted who would study where, Ha had no input in decisions that would affect her life. That was hard enough to take. But when she began to notice that the system appeared to have no clear match between the supply of people studying in a field and the demand for those skills in Vietnam, she became more discouraged. Why should she study Russian and then return to Vietnam? What would she do with it? With Portuguese she might have a chance at a diplomatic job and see the world.

In her assessment, Russia and Vietnam as its partner, were wasting human resources. In her thinking this happened "because of willful determination and preplanned decisions about goals that may fit nowhere with societal needs." Spoken like a person beginning to wonder about choice.

Later on, Ha discovered just how right she was. Of the several dozen Vietnamese university students she knew in Russia at the time, only one subsequently pursued a career in the field that he studied. The others, like Ha, were told to study a discipline that they never used in their careers, which were also chosen for them. The result: no match between their supply of skills and the demand for those skills. This was the Planned Economy in action.

But Ha's education did not end there. Like other Vietnamese students abroad, she knew her family expected her to be a "savior" and find ways to earn money that she could send home. She watched other Vietnamese students make money by taking Vietnamese made t-shirts, jeans, perfume and lipstick into Russia and reselling them. Those saviors whispered to one another, "Carry this to Russia. The trading ring will know how to find you. Just get your money, and then buy things others tell you to and bring them back to Vietnam." Trading 101.

But even as her mind was opening to ideas of supply and demand, Ha was a strong believer in socialist tenets and wanted to earn money in "appropriate" ways. Trading and business were not appropriate. Karl Marx had made that clear and Ha wanted no part of the evil that trading conveyed.

So there she was. No choice in what to study, no choice in where to study, and now pressure to trade, which for her was evil. Resist or join the others; trade and be her family's "savior" or find another way? Tough choice.

Think About It: *How and when did you learn about how to make choices in your life? And when did you ever you face a choice that meant going against some strongly held belief? How did you analyze and reach a decision?*

- learned Choices early w/ dad being so sick
- moved out 18
- Support self since then but perhaps even younger.

Part II

WHY WE WORRY

PART II: WHY WE WORRY

> *What I worry about most, and I think everybody should be worried about too, is Vietnam's weak 'cultural spirit capability' (bản lĩnh văn hóa). When dealing with international communities, clashes of economic interests or politics, appear, but the underlying clashes are socio-cultural in nature. The invasion of dominating cultures imported from alien systems and territories can cause more deep and detrimental impacts on the Vietnamese than any other type of invasion (war, economics). [To fight this], Vietnamese need an absolute trust in their own country, their people. But to me it seems this core trust has been eroding and become rusty, or even depraved, over time.*
>
> Ngô Phuong Chi
> Senior manager
> State Capital Investment Corporation

As we mentioned at the start of the book, Vietnam is at a fork in the road. It has long held traditions and ways of operating that are facing threats—from the outside world and from changes that any market economy brings. In this section, we'll talk about several issues that cause us and others to worry for Vietnam. Some may be similar to what's happening in other emerging economies, like China or India, some may mirror what many countries are facing in these tumultuous economic times, and still others may be specific to Vietnam, as the quote above suggests.

Specifically we talk about the traditional cultural values' focus on hierarchy and the importance of relationships, including our concern about how such ideas may affect creativity and innovation from developing and how future leaders will learn and build their organizations. We'll also talk about the dangers of short-term thinking that has emerged in the country, perhaps limiting people from thinking about "big dreams." In addition, we will talk about how difficult it can be for people who have not lived in conditions of choice to learn what the nuances for a market economy might be, including the idea that with gain comes risk and what that can bring. Finally, and in conjunction with the idea of individual choice, we discuss how challenging it is to change from a mindset of herd to independent thinking. If people are unable to make that shift, what might that mean for the future competitiveness of the country?

Cracks in traditional values?

Several years ago, the *Vietnam News,* Vietnam's government-owned English language newspaper, reported on a contest open for teenagers throughout the country. The contest was to come up with the most creative ideas to solve two of the country's biggest problems:

1. how to reduce the increasing levels of air pollution, especially in large cities
2. how to get clean water to every part of the country.

The prize money would be $2,500 for each of the students who came up with the best ideas.

Now let's put that winning prize money into context. At the time, the average annual income of a Vietnamese family was about $1,000. In the cities, it was a bit more, in the countryside, a bit less. But if we use $1,000 as a rough estimate, then think about the impact of that prize money on any young person considering entering the contest. A winning idea could provide prize money that might double a student's family yearly income. Significant impact, indeed.

When Nancy read about the contest, she reacted like many foreigners (and perhaps Vietnamese) had. First, the fact that the government was asking for input, for creative new ideas from the public and from teenagers no less, was remarkable. That's a common practice in other parts of the world, but not so much in Vietnam. It raised the question of whether the government was indeed serious about asking younger people for ideas, in a society that for so much of its history assumed that elders had the wisdom to solve problems. Or was the contest a foreign aid initiated venture? Did it truly mean that the government was willing to reach outside its traditional ranks to ask for ideas?

Second, the amount of the prize money was astounding. Perhaps not large in a country like the U.S., but in relative terms, to offer money that would double a family's income meant the equivalent of perhaps $100,000 in the United States. Was this an indication that the Vietnamese officials saw creativity as important and valuable for the country's next phase of development?

Such a contest for teenagers to solve some of Vietnam's problem could suggest a direction that is new for the country. On the other hand, it could simply be a one-off event, more for public relations than to usher in a new movement toward encouraging creativity.

Think About It: *How could a country—or an organization—encourage new ideas in a way that is sustainable and not just a one-time opportunity? What is the reaction if a contest happens once and not again?*

*

*   *

Time, Vietnamese style

Many businesspeople may return from Japan or China or even Vietnam with stories of how long it takes to get things done. In our own business school classes, we use case discussions about how crafty the Japanese can be in "using" time against the impatient American: taking days and weeks to negotiate a contract that would take hours in the U.S. Some Americans may finally give in more than they'd anticipated simply because they need to "catch a flight home." In Vietnam, Nancy was constantly surprised that a task her Vietnamese university colleagues said was almost finished could take a year or more.

As Nguyên Si Dung, Office of the National Assembly, Deputy Head, has commented: "Vietnamese have a habit of taking actions at the very last minute, leaving no possibility to adjust to mounting pressures." By following such a pattern, they may operate in ways that much of the western world does not and perhaps miss opportunities.

Nancy experienced that frequently. Often, when Nancy was working with colleagues, they would tell her that she had to give a presentation or attend a very important dinner an hour before the event. They rarely prepared for classes or a meeting ahead of time, which can be stressful for their "let's get it done early" foreign colleagues. It did not allow for "simmering" of ideas, for improving and making changes because they were simply scurrying to get something prepared. And the reasons for "wait till the last minute?"

"We know the information will change or the event will be cancelled so why prepare?"

"I have no control over my life, because others tell me what to do. By not responding or preparing until the last possible moment, I'm in control."

"Withholding information is powerful. My boss never tells me till the last minute, giving me no chance to react. So I have power if I don't tell you until the last minute."

That attitude of time may also help explain the lack of a long-term perspective. Many Americans might assume that, because Vietnam was long a "planned economy," and because it has a long history, its people may have a good notion of planning and a long-term perspective. Not so. In fact, "planning," in the planned economy sense meant primarily that state owned enterprises were told how much steel or electricity or shirts to produce, not how to plan for what might be demanded. That may also help explain the lack of a long-term perspective. If no one learned to plan or to think about consequences of a plan, there is no need to think long term.

As Ngô Phuong Chi with the State Capital Investment Corporation says, "I know it is extremely difficult for Westerners in this situation, especially when the long term vision of the West may not match with short term business interests sought after by the locals." Even though American firms often perform in the "short term," to meet quarterly performance objectives, this seems different. Long term for U.S. firms in this context would refer to investment opportunities.

Chi sees these perspectives—short term on the part of the Vietnamese and long(er) term on the part of Western business managers—as a "diametrical difference," especially since Vietnamese assume the foreigners who want to enter the local market and work with Vietnamese know about the rule *"nhập gia tùy tục"*—meaning, when joining a family, one has to observe its rules/customs. Chi also sees that short-term thinking and quick shifting creates "muddled and inconsistent policymaking and mushrooming of special interest groups that dominate economic life of the country, compromising the public welfare."

Yet, even though it is frustrating, Chi thinks the "short-term-ness" may have benefits. Such flexibility, as it were, could help Vietnamese be more dynamic and able to adjust to changing environments. If they could tap it, perhaps it would help them learn faster how to "address many seemingly unsolvable problems." Maybe, according to Chi, the foreign businesspeople could "invest in an important exercise: persuading and educating the Vietnamese about the values of long-term commitment and strategic plans."

What an interesting way to turn a "worry" into a "hope!"

Short-term thinking, small dreams?

We small guys sleep on narrow beds
Our small dreams crush our little fates.

Chê Lan Viên (1920-1989)
Nguoi di tim hinh cua nuoc, written in 1960

The Trung Nguyên Coffee Group's founder and owner, Dang Lê Nguyên Vu, worries that short-term thinking, like narrow beds, may make for small dreams. Vu dreams big and has achieved many of those dreams. He built a coffee company and network of coffee houses that stretches throughout the country. In 2010, Vu challenged the country to reach an export target for the coffee industry: US$20 billion every year.

How big a challenge is his target? In 2012, Vietnam was the world's largest coffee exporter, with a revenue of US$3.67 billion, a long way from $20 billion. In fact, when Vu mentioned his target challenge at the 2010 Conference on Sustained Growth for Vietnam's Coffee Industry, most in the room laughed out loud. But not all. Dr. Dang Kim Son, Director of the Institute of Policy and Strategy for Agriculture and Rural Development (IPSARD), the think tank of Vietnam's Ministry of Agriculture and Rural Development, agreed. Even more, he mentioned the need for a well thought-out (long-term) strategy for achieving the target.

Sadly, as of 2013, the strategy for Vietnam's coffee industry is very likely a thick document idling in a governmental desk drawer. But Mr. Vu does not sit still. Even as Starbucks enters Vietnam, Vu has already built one coffee factory and acquired another from Vinamilk, the country's largest dairy producer, to raise his firm's production capacity. In addition, he has expanded into Asean countries, Japan, and Australia. Next stop: the United States. Vu believes in the power of coffee for creativity and responsibility (creating new values for the society's benefits instead of self-interest), but more on that in the next section about why we hope.

Think About It: *How can short term thinking limit your dreams?*

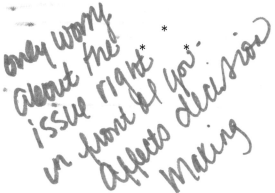

Who has the answers?

Where do I get ideas to solve problems? From myself, when I play golf. I cannot ask my peers, I cannot ask my subordinates. I cannot show doubt or weakness. I must find the answers myself.

CEO of a large Vietnamese insurance firm

The top leader of any organization has a lonely job. Chief Executive Officers, no matter what type of organization, often say that no one quite understands the job before doing it. So if top leaders want people to talk with about problems, they have a difficult choice to make. Who to go to?

The danger, of course, is that as a CEO has success, he will start to receive accolades—from within the organization or from the press outside. If he takes the press to heart, the CEO could begin to assume that he has the "right answers" and could also fall into a common situation where the CEO doesn't listen to alternative views and eventually weeds out people around him who may disagree. As those dissenting views disappear, an unfortunate result could be poorly thought through decisions, with no friction of discussion to strengthen them.

Some CEOs and senior leaders in organizations see such dangers, though, and deliberately try to find and vet different ideas. But to do so, they need at least two factors. First, they need people who can provide diversity of thinking who are willing and able to challenge the CEO. Some find or hire those people within their organizations. Others look outside the organization to peers who may be in different industries and could bring wildly different perspectives. Regardless, the CEOs seem to intentionally seek different viewpoints.

Second, the CEO must (learn to) not make quick judgments or shut down a discussion even if it is uncomfortable to hear. Even then the best leaders who try to be open to ideas and encourage employees to voice them can unconsciously send messages that go against that. A CEO of an organization that conscientiously seeks to be innovative once sat in a meeting with younger employees. An employee offered an idea and then watched the CEO lean back, lift an eyebrow, and cross his arms. He said nothing, but his posture and body language said everything. As the employee said later, "I'll never suggest a new idea to him again." In five seconds, the culture of innovation had a major chink in it, all because of a simple body gesture.

So it is difficult in the best of circumstances for ideas to emerge within organizations. But in Vietnam, where hierarchy and the expectation that wisdom comes from elders is so strong, what chance may creativity and innovation have in the future? Several reasons make it especially difficult for a Vietnamese CEO to ask for or test ideas inside or outside of his organization.

First, given the tradition and belief in hierarchy, people at all levels of an organization expect the person above to have answers. This means they will (or are expected to) show respect to people in positions higher than themselves. Remember the manager we talked about, who was so annoyed at the secretary who was not "respectful" when she came into an office, put papers on his desk, turned and left? Her actions challenged his belief of and expectations about hierarchy.

The same expectation comes up when it comes to finding ideas or solving problems. Employees look to their supervisors, supervisors look to middle managers, and middle managers look to the CEO for advice, direction and "answers" to questions. To suggest that the senior person doesn't "know" or have an answer would be heresy. Thus, those lower in the ranks expect it and those in the senior leaders know that if they show any doubt or lack of knowledge, they lose credibility. Result: the senior leader can never ask for input from those below.

Making the situation even more complicated, at any given level within an organization, a manager could never go to a peer for advice or input, because that would likewise be a sign of weakness or that the manager is not capable of handling a problem. Vietnamese are shocked when American or foreign managers ask for input on problems to be solved. They secretly think the manager is not credible or knowledgeable, but of course in other parts of the world, managers have learned that diverse ideas and views can help with problem solving or finding different ways to get things done and improve performance. Not so in Vietnam. The manager would lose credibility among peers, even if those working for him never knew. For a CEO, of course, the situation would be even more tenuous because it would involve going outside of the organization perhaps to a counterpart, which could damage his reputation and that of the firm.

Think About It: *What role does country culture play in encouraging (or inhibiting) new ideas or solutions to problems? And how do leaders you know get information?*

*

*　　*

Gain is the opposite of risk

Dâu Thuy Ha, the young woman who went to Moscow hoping to study Portuguese but was sent elsewhere in Russia, to study Russian, began making choices about her life. She wanted to control her own destiny and discovered how difficult that could be.

When she and her husband returned to Vietnam, they needed work. Links through family and friends guided her to a vice minister who "introduced" Ha to the government system. She joined the Department of International Cooperation of Vietnam's Ministry of Agriculture, a dream job for most Vietnamese: it was a secure post with built in opportunities to travel abroad, which for most people meant a chance to enhance their incomes. She had watched her Vietnamese student colleagues in Russia find ways to make money and she knew that this new job could provide the same chances for her. But Ha chose to leave the dream job after four months, saying it was uninteresting and "unsuitable" for her new way of thinking, which meant making choices and, although she didn't think of it this way yet, taking risks.

Ha joined the South Korean *chaebol*, Daewoo, then located at No. 1 Ba Triêu Street, the most expensive location in the city's center. Just a few meters from Hoan Kiêm Lake, the location reeked of expected success. Daewoo also built one of Hanoi's most impressive and modern hotels on the western side of town, near embassies and expatriate living quarters. Its biggest claim to fame: a banana shaped swimming pool, striking in its originality but not practical for swimmers who had to swim in a curve.

In her five years at Daewoo, Ha learned key lessons: "Never leave the office before your boss; focus completely on a task, and argue but then once a decision is made, support it to your best ability." She stopped working at 8

PM, just like her boss. She watched Korean colleagues focus on the job during the day, and then relax in the evening, a stark contrast to the Vietnamese relaxed approach during the day, where employees tried to look busy while having little to do and took two hours for lunch. She also watched Daewoo managers and staff argue about a decision, accept the final decision and then come together to implement it.

Then Ha made another atypical choice. She joined an American firm, and met Americans for the first time. Her memories of 30 April 1975, Liberation Day from the Americans couldn't have been far away. In 1996, Ha became the third employee of Hewlett-Packard in Vietnam, a firm with a name that was difficult for Vietnamese to pronounce. If Daewoo taught Ha how decisions were made and implemented in a military fashion, HP taught her efficiency and management expertise.

"For the first time in my life I heard about a personal development plan—how to set goals, how to be evaluated and reviewed." The concept offered Ha both freedom and accountability. Naturally, she set two personal goals right away: to pursue a masters degree in Business Administration and to set up her own firm before she turned 40. She had ten years to go.

HP paid her well, and Ha soon began to worry about "living too long in a comfort zone." She completed her MBA in 1999 and worked for HP for three years to repay the firm for supporting her degree program. Now she had one more goal, to open her own firm: with her degree she had the theory; with her time at Daewoo and HP, she had the experience. She was willing to take a risk. What else did she need?

As Ha looks back, she realizes now just how naïve she was. But then, the time seemed right. Vietnam's legislature approved a new Enterprise Law that would support small enterprises. The law's effective date—1 January 2000—

represented a new century and millennium, and as a firm believer in the importance of dates, Ha saw the law and its date as a symbol. She had visited her fortune teller and he confirmed the signs were good for a new opportunity.

Ha opened her new venture in 2002 and four months later, the firm collapsed. The obvious cause was "tough economic conditions," of course. But Ha doesn't go in for easy excuses and says the theory she learned failed in practice. Or perhaps the theory was right, but as a new manager, she was unable to turn it into practice. Running a business was far different from planning it, no matter how smart and well organized she was.

A colleague from Hewlett-Packard heard learned of the disaster, called Ha and offered her a job if she wanted to return. That would have been a safe option, a way of regrouping and reassessing next steps. But Ha refused the offer, largely because of the obligation to people who had joined her in the new firm. Deep in her Confucian thinking, she knew that asking someone for help obligates you to the person in the future. She could not leave those who had joined her venture and accepted its risk. The solution was to rebuild.

In time, Ha took another risk and created another firm. But this time, she built a "nano-sized" firm, not even big enough to be considered "small." Organizational Consultants Development was born in April 2003, and offered management consulting services, training and development. The firm received contracts and grew. Then, once again, disaster hit. In 2007, messy management practices and conflict among the partners split the firm. Ha kept a few loyal colleagues and the OCD brand, and started once again, in 2008. It took yet another year to stabilize, but then, once again, in 2011, the company faltered, despite the knowledge and experience Ha and other managers had gained by then. Ha's daughter, reaching an age where college was on the horizon, watched as her mother used their family's savings and strength of will to keep her firm going.

But strength of will and financial underpinnings were still not enough. Ha's latest scare taught her yet another lesson that macro-economic conditions can sap a firm's cash more quickly and in a devastating way than expected. Ha now insures that the firm always maintains a financial cushion, equivalent to three months of payroll, cash (at home or in the bank). After risking so much, her venture is finally stable and she is reaping gains. Too often, however, Vietnamese take risks without acknowledging the chance for failure.

Think About It: *When have you assumed that a risk would pay off? When have you assumed it might fail? Why? How did you learn to assess risk?*

*

*   *

Am I as ready as I think I am?

Over the years, in his work ranging from the World Bank/International Finance Corporation (IFC) to his own firms, Hoang interviewed numerous job applicants. A key task was to assess their "readiness," in the broadest sense of the word, for the jobs they sought.

In only a few cases did the perception (on the part of the applicant) of readiness match Hoang's assessment. For example, a young woman who was shortlisted for an administrative assistant position at IFC met the requirements on academic achievement and language skills. When asked if she was ready to apply her English and other language skills in business communication tasks, she replied immediately that she was ready. The next step in the process was a test— she was to write a short letter to arrange a meeting for her potential boss with a Vietnamese CEO. She was told that both men were extremely busy, would not be interested in a long letter, but that the Vietnamese CEO needed some basic information on the IFC mission to decide whether to meet with the IFC boss. Sadly, the test revealed that the applicant was unable to frame such a letter, even in her own Vietnamese language, let alone in English. Some 30 minutes after her confident "I am ready" statement, the applicant withdrew her candidacy. As she said to Hoang, "I am not ready for *this* particular task," but still was confident that, given other assignments, she could excel. Needless to say, she never received a job at the IFC.

Another example comes from the world of manufacturing, which we might expect is one of Vietnam's strong areas, given lower labor costs and high unemployment. During a search for a possible factory to construct folding chairs for a U.S.-based firm, Trần Tri Dung (Managing Partner for DHVP) discovered the process was not as straightforward as he hoped. In 2011, Dung searched for six months to find a reliable and quality manufacturer to make the chairs at a lower cost than Chinese rivals. He learned that either the manufacturing facilities could not meet expected quality standards or, if they could, none of the facilities wanted the business.

Further, in 2013, the popular online newspaper *VnExpress* reported that world leaders in mobile phones (e.g., Nokia and Samsung) had tried to staff up their facilities in Vietnam and had a very difficult time. Samsung Electronic Vietnam, for instance, received 20,000 job applications for a particular job; only 3,000 were qualified and the company finally hired 1,200.

As Dung suggests, a ~~fundamental concern is whether young people—perhaps all Vietnamese—have a capacity to think clearly, logically, and systematically about the future.~~ As diplomat Nguyên Trung Thanh has said, Vietnam "is moving into an uncharted water, and current and next generations of Vietnamese will have to explore, learn and plan on their own."

In the past, the principle method that Chinese and Vietnamese have used during transition has been more intuitive and slow. According to Thanh, an approach of "crossing the river by feeling the stones" (摸着石头过河 – "*dò đá qua sông*") has dominated. When a person is skeptical about crossing a river, he throws stones with each step to judge the depth or any dangers. If all seems safe, then he moves forward, step by step. Such a philosophy of "gradualism" may have worked in earlier times, but as the pace and environment change rapidly, is that the best approach going forward? To Dr. Nguyên Si Dung of the National Assembly, ~~this "gradualism" may no longer be good enough in a much faster changing world as it is today. Rising pressures caused by increasing pace of the globalization process, especially international trade and financial integration, have become a source of worry if the country cannot keep up its institutional reforms in the coming years—another aspect of "readiness," this time for the country as a whole.~~

Think About It: *What approach could people use in fast changing times? How will students and others change their thinking, if needed, from one of intuition to one that includes more systematic and logical approaches?*

*
*   *

What's in it for me?

An ancient Greek mathematician became well known for his rigorous proofs in plane geometry. One day a wealthy businessman came to the mathematician and asked to be taken on as a student. The mathematician agreed and then gave the businessman his geometry book to read. After three days, the businessman made little progress: he just could not get motivated to learn the complex arguments and logic of geometry. So he returned to the famous mathematician with a different request. As we imagine it, the comment would go like this: "Sir, this knowledge is really complex and difficult, so to help me be motivated to learn it, tell me what benefit I will gain after reading this. I need to know what's in it for me to become motivated to do it."

The mathematician refused to respond, but the businessman (being a good businessman) persisted. Then finally, the mathematician turned to his assistant and said: "My student, since this man wants some 'benefit' for completing the reading, please give him three cents." As the story goes, the businessman was satisfied and went off to complete his assignment.

Many Vietnamese say that the happiest day for them every month is payday. In a money-driven society, where people seek only money, will they drop their dreams or ethical standards, and assume money will bring them happiness? We see some young people, including college students who do not earn money while they are studying, use their parents' money on beer, entertainment or personal devices (iPhones, iPads), and less on learning. Indeed, even though statistics have long claimed that Vietnam has one of the region's highest literacy rates, people seem to be reading less and less. According to Gian Tu Trung, founder of the business training firm PACE, Vietnamese read only 0.8 book a year—less than *one* book a year. And what might that mean for the country's ability to participate in the global economy going forward?

Likewise, if payday is so important, and money is king, many people worry that the ultimate problem is corruption, especially when there is no effective way to avoid it. Dr. Lê Xuân Dinh, one of Hoang's friends and Editor-in-Chief of the *Economy and Forecast Review*, has that worry himself.

> *The public media has mentioned that bribery accounts for 1-5% of business costs. The problem of corruption will remain until personal incomes are well governed. In other words, the country needs to reinforce 'income security.' Good government of personal income will not only increase the state's revenue but make issues of politics, economics, society and even national security transparent and accountable.*

Think About It: *What drives your behavior? Is it making money? If people do not feel "secure" in their income levels and resort to corruption, how does Vietnam stop the cycle?*

From fried eggs to a business degree: Illusions and curses of education

The quality of higher education in Vietnam is perceived to be so low that some claim "only the poor will let their children study in domestic universities." Those able to send their children abroad do so to the U.S., England, Europe, or Japan. Some even send them to Thailand, although some professors there question the quality of local universities as well. Professor Dolly Samson, Stamford University, Bangkok, claims that Thai education is suspect due to rampant plagiarism and double standards, allowing students of powerful and rich parents to glide through.

The tension between money and education comes up in other ways. A Belgian professor has spent 15 years in Vietnam's higher education system and has seen many changes in the economy through the lens of the classroom. He worked for an internationally recognized Australian university that has campuses in both Hanoi and Saigon. Tuition is about $30,000/year and his students reflect it: many young women wear name brand dresses, carry Louis Vuitton bags, use Macbook Air laptops, and drive expensive cars. His worry, however, comes not from the fact that the students have money, but rather how it seems to influence the perception of education.

One day in a class on public institution administration, the professor noticed a student who was completely engrossed in her iPad. He asked what distracted her so much from his lecture. (Granted, all of us who teach hope that our lectures are so engaging nothing would distract our students. Alas, too often we fail.)

At least she was honest.

"Oh, I am frying eggs on my iPad. It is a new app."

Given her rich parents, it was likely she would skim through the university. In the professor's view, the young student was "frying eggs for a business degree."

When he retired, Professor Dam Van Nhuê, former head of the Faculty of Post-Graduate Studies at the well-regarded National Economics University (NEU) in Hanoi, joined a private university—which had been founded by Professor Trân Phuong. Professor Phuong was a former Deputy Prime

Minister of Vietnam just right before *Doi Moi* began (in 1986). He is the author/architect of "price-wage-currency" reforms—known in Vietnamese as "Giá-Lương-Tiền" incident—in 1985 that pushed the Vietnamese economy to a widespread chaotic situation. Nhuệ's salary at the private university was much higher than it had been at the NEU, and as he has said, the "high pay came from students' parents." In fact, the university's President explains this "philosophy" to new professors who join: remember that the parents are the reason for your salary, thus, if anyone is to be expelled that should be salary-receiving professor, never fee-paying students.

Think About It: How do you and others in your country view, scorn or value education? Why?

*
*   *

China: The northern giant

China clearly influences Vietnam, from Confucianism to cultural values and customs to political ideology. However, fighting against the northern giant's dominance has been a Vietnamese struggle for more than a thousand years, despite the many Chinese characters on signs in front of shops, hotels and restaurants. Instead, Vietnamese people, implicitly and explicitly, dislike Chinese people. Chinese tourists are seen as noisy, messy, and haughty. On the other hand, as the

Vietnamese learn to do business, they realize that the Chinese demand is just too big to ignore.

Yet, even as the Vietnamese love Chinese-style food, the art of cooking and range of spices, they view products and food from China with suspicion, and tell their children to be wary as well. The Vietnamese view Chinese products as low in quality, and often teach their children that "made-in-China" toys are dangerous or harmful. Vietnamese fear receiving poisoned Chinese fruits and food and thus, many Vietnamese women refuse to buy fruit from China.

Given the rising tension in the South China Sea, called the East Sea in Vietnam, Vietnamese politicians are officially pursuing "a friendly neighborhood," a sort of communist brotherhood, while perhaps they fully recognize the public's anger and wariness about Chinese aggressiveness.

Nevertheless, China is a major trading partner of Vietnam. Bilateral trade grew more than 20% per year between 2009 and 2012 period, doubling in value (from $21 billion to $41 billion), as Vietnam's deficit with China jumped from $11.5 billion in 2009 to $16.4 billion in 2012. In addition, Chinese contractors often beat Vietnamese rivals for contracts inside Vietnam, largely because of Vietnamese bidding policies which favor cheaper offers.

But despite tensions, the Vietnamese know they need to interact with the Chinese and are learning, even as they push against dominance and the undercurrent of skepticism remains.

*

*　　*

Will Vietnamese trust themselves?

We started this section with a quote from Ngô Phuong Chi about his fear that the invasion of other cultures into

Vietnam may weaken the Vietnamese identity. His fuller comment was that "without a clear identity and strong 'cultural spirit capability,' Vietnamese could easily be turned in to South Koreans, Japanese or Chinese, depending upon who has the more influential cultural capability."

Chi's fear is interesting and very likely valid. While the Vietnamese will proudly declare that even though the Chinese dominated for 1000 years, the Vietnamese retained and fought to keep their own language and culture. Chi seems to fear that this time around the invasion of many different cultures could greatly damage the country. At one extreme, some argue that the Vietnamese "believe everything done by foreigners is great." Without a strong sense of identity, could the Vietnamese be tugged and pulled in directions that fray its core? Is the process of trying out new ideas from different cultures one that will make the Vietnamese stronger or simply water down what has been fundamental in the past?

Even more damning, Chi suggests that unpredictable shifts in policy and direction may lead foreigners to distrust Vietnam in the future. If others cannot count on stable conditions, why would they wish to become business, educational or governmental partners? The result: if the Vietnamese do not believe in their own values, why should foreigners trust them?

We agree. We worry the Vietnamese need to trust themselves, to know themselves and to believe in themselves as the country moves forward. In the next section, however, we will talk about some characteristics that the Vietnamese do show that may help the country find its way in its own way.

Think About It: *What are the fundamental values in Vietnam that are important to maintain and be sure are consistently displayed? What would the equivalent be in America? How can each group be sure those values are clear?*

Part III

WHY WE HOPE

PART III: WHY WE HOPE

> *The union of Vietnam's people is the nation's strength. When Vietnam is united, not only internal resources… but also external resources converge on the development process for a beautiful, prosperous and peaceful Vietnam.*
>
> Dr. Lê Xuân Dinh, Editor-in-Chief
> *Economy and Forecast Review,*
> Ministry of Planning and Investment

Despite, or perhaps because of, the messy complexities, paradoxes, and challenges of Vietnam, we do have hope for the country. We rest that hope on several elements others and we have hinted at throughout the book.

We are hopeful first because of three fundamental characteristics that the Vietnamese people have exhibited and used for generations. As a group, the Vietnamese have repeatedly shown they are resourceful, resilient, and able to reinvent—themselves and their country. Time after time, when the Vietnamese have been resource-less, they find ways to become resource-full, whether in fixing equipment, solving a problem, or finding food when it was scarce. Their resilience, likewise, comes through in how people adjust, accept, and then know where to push on an issue. As many Vietnamese say, we are calm and relaxed but when we are pushed too far, we become unbeatable fighters. Last, the Vietnamese, as individuals and as a country, survived and thrived when they have reinvented themselves. Like people in any turmoil or unpredictable situation, that's a requirement of survival.

Finally, we are also hopeful because of the possibilities we see emerging in the bridge generation, including Hoang and many of the people we have quoted in this book: younger leaders who have lived through war and hard economic times, who have watched *Doi Moi* market renovation fits and starts and who are moving into positions of regional and global importance. With their vision, energy and creativity, watch out world, here comes the new Vietnam.

Resourcefulness

In 1971, the American War was in full force. So when Bach Ngoc Chiên was born, his parents wanted to give their first son a strong name that would help him through life. They chose the name Chiên, which meant "The Fighter." Their second son, Du, born in 1973, was named after his mother's favorite writer, Nguyên Du. A final son, born in 1975, arrived after the war ended, so they named him "An," which means "peace." The Fighter took his name to heart, which was a good thing since he would need the spunk that it brought him throughout his life.

One day in 1981, the local pig trader arrived, when ten-year-old Chiên and his two younger brothers were tending their family's pigs. The boys had responsibility to make sure the pigs had enough to eat, did not wander off, and were healthy and ready for market, when the pig trader arrived. The boys' mother normally welcomed and negotiated price with the pig trader but that day, she was working in the rice fields so young Chiên took charge. He knew that the trader determined the price based upon a pig's weight when it was still alive, which meant making sure the pigs were as heavy as he could before she weighed them. Chiên and his brothers decided to trick the pig trader, but they needed to buy time.

Chiên kept the trader distracted, telling her stories—about the history of his village's name, about his family—whatever seemed to capture and hold the trader's attention for a few minutes longer. Meanwhile, eight-year-old Du and six-year-old An cooked a light soup and fed the pigs as much as they could.

The pig trader, a veteran businesswoman, saw through the ruse but rather than being angry, she told the boys' mother that the family should be proud of the three sons who would bring luck and prosperity to the family.

Think About It: *When was the last time you had to be resource-full when you were resource-less? What did you learn from it?*

It's not just children who find ways to be resource-full. Stories of leaders show the same ability. Vo Van Kiêt, who became one of Vietnam's most respected Prime Ministers, presided over Hô Chi Minh City after the American War ended. The possibility of famine was real because of the shortage of rice. So by 1979, when he was Secretary of HCMC's Party Committee, he founded a "rice smuggling task force." The task force was sent to Mekong Delta River, the country's rice bowl, to buy rice at market prices (which was illegal), transport the rice to Hô Chi Minh City (also illegal), and sell the rice to people living in the city (illegal too).

The actions thus reduced the price and increased the supply of rice. Yes, illegal, but Vo Van Kiêt saw bigger gains, such as decreasing the risk of famine, that were worth the chance of arrests. In fact, he said that if someone was imprisoned for smuggling, he would take food to the prisoners himself while they were incarcerated. The result: people of HCMC had enough to eat and the city went on to become the commercial hub for the country.[12]

Vo Van Kiêt was not alone in taking risks. In 1966, during the buildup of the American War, Kim Ngoc (1917-2012), a Vinh Phuc provincial party chief, went against the direct orders of then General Secretary Lê Duân to *de facto* privatize land use rights to farmers. This was during a time when the Communist Party sought to "co-operatize" farm land. Yet, Kim Ngoc realized the potential for de-motivation of the farmers with such a scheme, which would only lead to lower productivity and output of agriculture products, which the country sorely needed. So he quietly experimented with allowing farmers to maintain land use rights and more self-determination, hoping that the actions would increase efficiency. In the process, he took all responsibility himself for the consequences of defying the General Secretary's orders.

In fact, productivity and yield soared. Still, the party leaders condemned Kim Ngoc and ordered him to stop his experiments, which at that point he had to do. He waited for the discipline that was bound to come to him. But, surprisingly, it did not. So Kim Ngoc quietly "transferred" his policies to other provinces, receiving many thanks from farmers who benefitted. The experiments ultimately became the start of the agricultural reforms in Vietnam during *Doi Moi*, and moved the country out of famine. Today, Vietnam is one of the top three exporters of rice in the world,

---

[12]Dang Phong (2008). "To buon lau gao cua bi thu thanh uy," *Tuoi tre*, Jun. 15. <http://tuoitre.vn/Tuoi-tre-cuoi-tuan/263324/to-buon-lau-gao-cua-bi-thu-thanh-uy.html>

perhaps in part because someone was willing to take a risk and be resource-full.

> **Think About It:** *Can you think of any examples of leaders—government, business or other—who have taken a risk for a greater good?*

*

*   *

Resilience and the Four F's

Any Vietnamese or American over 40 years old can remember something about the war between the two countries. Older Vietnamese can recount numerous losses— family members and friends who died, who became and remain missing in action, families split by arbitrary borders, by ideology, and in some cases, by an ocean between the refugees who fled and family members who remained in the country. Needless to say, Americans did not have good street credibility or respect from Vietnamese for years.

Americans, as well, felt bruised, if not trampled and crushed, by years of friction in the U.S. about the war, about the experience of being in Vietnam or knowing people who were. Many have refused, even 50 years later, to talk about or acknowledge a country that caused so much pain for them.

But that began to change, on both sides, in the 1990s and 2000s. One of the most vivid examples of how people on opposite sides of the war can change their views comes from the story of a young Vietnamese physician, whose diaries talked about the war in personal terms that touched many hearts.

Dr. Dang Thuy Trâm worked as a doctor in northern Vietnam during 1968-1970, when the American War was at its zenith. Dr. Trâm wrote in several diaries about her life as a young doctor in the field, of her desire for the love of a good man, and of her strong feelings for her country and the war that kept her from her family.

Trâm died on 22 June 1970, in the central province of Quang Ngai, one of the deadliest battlefields during the war. The circumstances are unclear but the presumption is that American soldiers shot Trâm and her colleagues as they walked out of the Ba To mountain area. After any death, the standard American military procedure was to burn all non-military related papers. As Frederic Whitehurst, a young American intelligence specialist began the task, his Vietnamese translator, Nguyên Trung Hiêu, said, "Don't burn this [diary]. It contains fire already." Although it was against the rules, Whitehurst kept the small hand written notebooks, returned to the U.S. and stored them, still without knowing what they contained.

The diaries did not return home to Vietnam for more than thirty years.

In the U.S., years after the war, Whitehurst at last had the diaries translated and realized how much fire and emotion they held. He asked a colleague to track down Trâm's family in Hanoi and return the diaries. Whitehurst, however, was reluctant to have anything to do with the country, the family or returning. When the Trâm family published the diaries in April 2005, they became a sensation in Vietnam, selling 300,000 copies immediately. The title was *Last night, I Dreamed of Peace (Đêm qua, tôi mơ thấy hòa bình)*. The revered military strategist and leader, General Vo Nguyên Giap, who led the Vietnamese in their defeat of both the French and the Americans, presented Dr. Trâm's family with a medal of honor.

Later in 2005, Whitehurst did at last visit Vietnam, fighting the reluctance and emotion he had about the country and his experiences during the war. He was doubtless unnerved at the thought of meeting the family of the young doctor who had died so long ago. Yet Trâm's family welcomed him, took him to the battlefield where their daughter and sister died. In the process, the family showed the characteristics of so many resilient Vietnamese who have lived through war and hardships.

The characteristics come up so often, they could be called the Four F's: never forget, try to forgive, make friends with your enemies—in this case, an American who was responsible for a relative's death—and look to the future. Their view of the West, and of America in particular, focuses more on finding ways to become partners going forward, not in holding grudges about what happened in the past.

Much later, Nancy and her colleague Trân Tri Dung sat in the Trâm family's living room with Trâm's mother, Mrs. Doan Ngoc Trâm and two of her three living daughters, Mrs. Dang Phuong Trâm and Mrs. Dang Kim Trâm, who were in their late fifties. We had come at the invitation of Mrs. Vo Hoa Binh, good friend of the Tram family and daughter of General Vo Nguyên Giap. Along a wall of the living room sits an altar that holds incense, flowers and fruit, along with photos of relatives who have died, including Dr. Trâm, her father and brother.

When Nancy asked the ladies what they thought Vietnam could teach the rest of the world, they said, almost in one voice, that "Vietnamese can even make friends with their former enemies, and do it quickly." After 100 years of colonization, the Vietnamese defeated the French in 1954 (thanks to General Giap, among others). Just two years later, France and Vietnam reestablished diplomatic relations and worked on joint economic, educational and political ventures. Japan, which occupied Vietnam during World War II, also later became diplomatic allies of the Vietnamese. Even with China, which dominated Vietnam for 1,000 years and has had border skirmishes on and off for years, Vietnam has forced a workable—if often tense—relationship.

Yet, after the U.S. withdrew from Vietnam in 1975, it took twenty years before diplomatic relationships reemerged. When you look at the numbers affected on each side, it's sometimes hard to understand how the Vietnamese could have the attitude of making friends with their enemies. In the war, nearly 60,000 Americans died; about 2500 were missing in action. The Vietnamese lost some three million people and had an estimated 300,000 MIAs. It's hard to imagine that forgiveness and moving forward are possible, but most Vietnamese have done it.

As Mrs. Binh says, "When we are at war, we cannot improve the country. And we have been a poor underdeveloped country for a very long time. If our energy goes to war, that means we cannot put it into developing the country."

"Spoken like the daughter of a general," said Mrs. Phuong Trâm.

True, but Mrs. Binh should know. Her father, General Giap, knew well the impact of war and wept when he read Dr. Trâm's diaries. And as Mrs. Binh says, "that's why we Vietnamese are good at forgiving. We want peace because we have for so many years experienced the devastating effects that wars have caused."

She has a point. In the 2013 rankings of the global peace index, Vietnam rates higher than any other country in Asia, except for Japan and Taiwan, much higher than its neighbors

Buddhist dominated Thailand or the Muslim dominated Indonesia.[13]

When, in the early 1990s, as American and Vietnamese began to meet again face to face, many American asked what the Vietnamese thought of them. The response was always the same, almost verbatim to what the Tram women and Mrs. Binh had said: "We never forget but try to forgive, we can even make friends with our enemies and look to the future." Ms. Binh added, "as to American veterans who return to Vietnam with peaceful goodwill, we want to heal the wounds (of both Vietnamese and Americans) and warmly welcome them."

Think About It: When is the last time you forgave, made friends and moved toward the future with a person or people that you have fought with— not necessarily in war, but in work or at home? How did you do it?

Reinvention

Nghiêm Phu Kiên Cuong was born in 1971, the fifth in a family of seven children. His oldest sibling was born in 1957, youngest in 1979. His home was at the Canh Crossroads, a name familiar to many Hanoians. It is the Vân Canh commune, in Hoai Duc district, near Hanoi. This region has

---

[13]Institute for Economics and Peace's GPI data, 2012
http://www.guardian.co.uk/news/datablog/2013/jun/11/global-peace-index-2013

for long been known as the farming suburbs supplying vegetables, food for Hanoi. Cuong's father, born in 1928, originally came from the nearby Tu Liêm district, on the western outskirts of Hanoi and his mother's silk trading family came from a small town known for weaving, called Ha Dông, about six miles from Hanoi. Both small towns have blended into Hanoi's metropolis, and instead of small farms or dirt roads, high rise apartments and luxury hotels have sprung up.

Both families had blemishes in their backgrounds from the 1940s, which no one could anticipate would hurt them decades later. The result: they had to reinvent.

In the 1940s, Cuong's paternal grandfather owned land, a lot of it. In fact, the family's plot was too large for the family to tend it alone so they hired local farmers to help to grow and sell vegetables. When the Viêt Minh took power in the northern part of Vietnam in 1945, however, the land was a liability. The government identified the family as part of the "landlord class," a label that hampered family members for years, and in the case of some of the children, for their lifetimes.

In a similar vein, Cuong's mother's family found itself in trouble. In traditional Vietnamese cultural values and in communist thought, conducting business and trade was seen as undesirable. Since Cuong's mother's family traded in silk, they were designated as "petite bourgeoisie," which even today still has a negative connotation for anyone applying for Communist Party membership or promotion to a key political post in a state agency, local or central government. So, to get along with the new government under Viêt Minh leadership, especially after the 1954 French defeat in Diên Biên Phu, Cuong's family on both sides relinquished their assets—land, gold and money—to the government. Even so, the "landlord class" and "petite bourgeoisie" labels stuck.

"Landlord" families were treated poorly, but Cuong's family avoided some difficulties thanks to one family member who became a war hero, of sorts. He joined the local militia before Independence Day, Sept 2, 1945, and was recognized for his contribution to the country's independence because he destroyed a French point guard on the outskirts of Hanoi during the Resistance War against the French. Because of that relative's action, Cuong's family was "relabeled" as a "landlord family joining the resistance war." That label gave them a safer haven in the North, for a short while.

But the family's luck continued to falter. After the French war ended in 1954, Cuong's father worked at the Huu Hung Brick Factory but unfortunately, fell out with some his colleagues, who fabricated a story about his mistakes at work. That led to his expulsion from the state-owned production operation, and two years in "rehabilitation camp." This event made Cuong's father learn more of the realities of life, and about what he could and could not do. But one thing he knew for sure was that he wanted his children to later become good citizens and that meant understanding how to be serious and hard workers.

Cuong's mother had worked in the state-run food distribution system since the mid-1950s, thanks to her family's expertise in trading. Her position gave the family a bit more access to food ration cards, and meant that the children had the status of being a dependent of a state employee. But then later, even that became a liability. In the 1950s and 1960s, people in the trading sector were seen as more versatile, resourceful and "smart," and unfortunately the label of being "smart" was negative, suggesting "profiteering," or that people in trade operations were ready to cheat others for their own gain.

By the late 1960s, Cuong's father was a man with no land, no job and a family with two children to support. So he began to act in ways that would much later become more popular in Vietnam: he was an entrepreneur before the concept arrived in Vietnam. Cuong's father saw how the economy was changing, especially in larger cities, and brought those ideas to his own town. Cuong thinks his father was the first person in Hoai Duc province to learn how to bake "*quy gai xôp*," a kind of biscuit that was popular in Hanoi, and was made from eggs, low quality flour and sugar. Because of the food shortage, many people faced malnutrition and so the sweet taste of sugar in the biscuits was a luxury. The *quy gai xôp* biscuit disappeared by the late 1980s, replaced by better tasting biscuits and cakes, but people born before 1980 still remember the old biscuits and the joy of a small bit of luxury. Cuong's father also learned how to make "*mỳ sợi*"—a low-quality dry noodle made of flour powder—that, for many years, replaced rice as major source of calories. The tradition of "*mỳ sợi*" noodles has continued with the popularity of instant noodles. The story of those early years became fodder for family stories and drove his children to understand that reinvention is part of life.

The late 1980s and early 1990s was a period ripe for new economic approaches in Vietnam and once again, Cuong's father showed the way. He exemplified the newly emerging "pavement economic model," and set up a tea corner, or "*quán trà*," on a sidewalk. The *quan tra* usually had a simple low-quality wooden table (normally very dirty), surrounded by a few wooden chairs or benches, or sometimes a tree stub that substituted for a chair. The owner bought products like cigarettes, tea, candy, and cakes and then resold them at the *quan tra* for just a little more, generating a "reasonable" margin. These small tea corners like the one that Cuong's father's started were part of what some Vietnamese called a "trading atom." Especially during the early 1990s as Vietnam moved from the all encompassing planned economy "toward a market oriented economy," the spontaneously developing pavement economic model offered a good way for people to learn about the market economy. Cuong watched and learned as well.

"My father has always been most influential to me. He worked very hard, always thinking of new opportunities to make money and teach his children to learn work skills and work attitude," said Cuong.

Think About It: When have you reinvented yourself? What conditions demand reinvention? Is it something that could be done even without hardship?

*

*　　*

One way reinvention occurs is through education, to be sure, and many leaders are guaranteeing that their children have every opportunity they can provide them. Like many Vietnamese parents who are able to afford it, *Dow Jones* journalist Nguyên Pham Muoi sent both of his children to American universities. His daughter, for instance, graduated from Columbia University, where she majored in political science. She represents the next generation of Vietnamese who will make a difference in how the world views Vietnam and how Vietnam views the world. As Muoi thinks about his children, and about the opportunities that they will have, he concludes:

"The most important thing for a nation is always having hope for the country, for the family, and for the people, especially for the future. To have that hope, every person has to know what the future can be and how to build it."

Yet not all Vietnamese have chosen the education route, and in fact, some find creative ways to "reinvent" themselves. Several years ago, Hoang's firm recruited a young woman who had left high school before finishing. Nguyên Thi Khanh Huyên joined the firm to work on a popular website that serves some 200,000 registered users, and has 3 million hits per month. One reason Ms. Huyên was so excited about joining was that there was no requirement to have a university degree, which was a good thing, because she had neither high school nor college credentials. But what she did have was English language skills, math skills and pluck. During the time she spent in high school, she had been in a program for students gifted in math and analytical skills and wanted to take advantage of that. But before finding a job, she wanted to travel. So she did.

By the time she returned, she was known as the daring young woman who traveled through 27 countries on $700. Her name and story inspired many young Vietnamese students and she wrote a book about her worldwide journey, giving credence to the notion that reinvention and taking charge of one's own life—whatever that decision may be—is possible, especially in the new Vietnam.

Huyên may be inspiration for young Vietnamese who value learning over formal education. A form of "self-education," where people learn by experiences that previously were unavailable, or through on line programs that bring them into contact with instructors and fellow learners from around the world, all of this is possible just in the period of a decade or two. Just as countries like Vietnam leap frogged technology, by passing land line phones and going directly to mobile phones, so too may they leap from traditional "chalk and talk" methods where the teacher lectures and delivers information, past the more "modern" Socratic educational approaches of using cases and discussion straight to new ways of education. Rather than attending the traditional, competitive and relationship-dependent Vietnamese universities, will younger people leave the country for universities abroad? Or, will they choose online educational programs, increasingly available anywhere? Or, will they forgo formal education and "credentials" altogether and just pursue self-learning?

Think About It: *What else could Vietnam leapfrog—other than technology and perhaps educational approaches—that would allow it to reinvent itself and surge ahead?*

*

* *

In 1994, an American banker stood in front of a group of Vietnamese faculty members, government and business employees to deliver a lecture about working capital. The room was fitted with equipment that ranged from an overhead slide projector to a Japanese air conditioner/heating unit, to creaky desks and wooden chairs. The 30 Vietnamese participants were ready to be taught.

"OK. Let's talk about working capital today, what it does for business firms, why it's useful, how you calculate it…."

Blank faces.

"Do you know why you *need* working capital?"

Blank faces.

"Do you know *what* it is?"

Blank faces.

"Do you know what *credit* is?"

Blank faces.

"Hmmm. Have you ever seen a credit card?" The banker pulled out a credit card from his wallet and held it up.

Blank faces, then smiles. It is tangible, has a picture on it, and some numbers.

"OK, that's where we will start."

Starting from the ground up, learning what business, markets, and entrepreneurial thinking means has been a short and furious process. Vietnam's first generation of formally recognized entrepreneurs started when the government approved the Enterprise Law. At the time, many people were not well educated, were unable to find jobs within government institutions (which to that point was considered a desirable occupation), so they needed to find other ways to earn money. The law gave them an opportunity to be acknowledged as an "economic player." The nature of early entrepreneurial ventures was primitive but the early stages allowed these budding players to gain critical know-how. One of the most crucial changes in thinking was the notion of investing—in people, inventory, product—before gaining revenue. Rather than working off a plan to produce and rather than meeting demand, the new entrepreneurs understood the market economy in much more tangible ways.

A second generation emerged in the early 2000s. Hoang, Ha and some of the other entrepreneurs we have mentioned exemplify the change and development of those second-generation entrepreneurs. Hoang and Ha, for instance, both were well-paid professionals at international institutions (the World Bank and Hewlett-Packard) in the 1990s. But each experienced a mental transformation from being passive participants to active creators in the new economy. At their prior jobs, they saw themselves as "receivers," who took instruction, did their best at work and waited for recognition from their bosses. With a change in mindset and as they moved into entrepreneurial ventures, they became shapers of their own destinies, where they generated jobs and revenue because of the quality of their firms' performance, not because of a planned output. More risky, more rewarding.

Their thinking shifted in other ways as well. They highly appreciate—and acknowledge publically—the contributions by their employees. In some cases, to eliminate the gap between "boss and employee," they don't even use the term "employee," but rather colleague, associate or partner, a very non-hierarchical and non-Confucian approach. They realize that while they must take ultimate responsibility for the success (or failure) of their firms, they know that the venture is not a one-person operation. They also have found that they cannot pay themselves as much as they would like (or as much as they made when they were "receivers") but the payoff is different, bigger, and more satisfying for them. Their attitudes are more "give now, take later."

And the next generation of entrepreneurs is coming just behind the bridge generation. Trần Trí Dung, managing partner of DHVP Research carries on the attitude—and, like so many others, looked to his parents for inspiration. His father and uncles were soldiers, sent to the southern fronts during the American War (and fortunately, all returned home). His father has long encouraged Dung to bring new friends—from America and elsewhere—to the house, where he can entertain and show them Vietnamese hospitality.

Dung also has seen his uncle, who survived one of the most fierce fights in Quang Tri during the American War, return home and study, and then teach, English. He understood, long before Dung did, that Vietnam would need to do business with the world outside and English was a pathway. Dung, too, realized the need to study topics that would help him become a global citizen. He chose international business at Hanoi National Economics

University in part because he saw business as "freedom," in how to spend his money and live his life, and a way to gain more opportunities. He has avoided the dangers of having too easy a life and expecting much from his parents. Instead, he's worked hard for any gains that the company has made.

Think About It: *Hungry entrepreneurs have been crucial to America's growth. Now they are helping to build Vietnam's. Could the two countries' entrepreneurs learn from each other or find ways to collaborate in business in the future?*

*

*   *

A country is similar to a man. He is born, grows, matures, ages, and dies. But the quality of the country in each phase is different from the others.

Bach Ngoc Chiên
Director, VTV4

With its greater connection to the world beyond its borders, Vietnam and its people are shifting in ways that may no longer be controllable. The internet, Facebook and social networks are ubiquitous, and more frequently used as places for voicing opinions as well as for learning new skills. New information, data, knowledge and insights are available and young people know that from now going forward, they cannot live without such access. Perhaps without fully realizing it, such access may be making them more open, responsive, and appreciative of modern cultural values that they never recognized before.

In addition, as people are more willing to express personal opinions, many are becoming more outspoken. Some criticism of policies and problems has become more frequent and somewhat "acceptable" to the public and for some in government. Other implications are emerging as well. Social networks may yield a new kind of civil society, with less need for policing or censorship because the "policing" is done by society in general. Plagiarism is more often uncovered, destroying careers and reputations of previously high-level scientists and researchers, but again, the result may be better work and more transparent development of information.

Finally, will the internet and social networks lead citizens to realize that they may have more control over the country's fate than relying solely on government or party direction? An example of how this may work happened in March 2013 when the Communist Party and National Assembly proposed a program to gather public opinion about changes in the Constitution of 1992. While leaders wanted a quick process, social networks changed the speed and the closed nature of the process. Many movements emerged to "help improve" the Constitution, including Vietnamese scientists living abroad, such as the mathematician Ngô Bao Châu, winner of the Fields Medal. The climax of the efforts was "Proposal 72," submitted to the National Assembly's unit in charge of amendments. The "72" refers to 72 famous and influential Vietnamese intellectuals, including world-renowned professor of mathematics Hoang Tuy and the writer Nguyên Ngoc, as well as the former Minister of Justice, Nguyên Dinh Lôc. The proposal requested the removal of Article 4, which stated that the Community Party is the only and supreme political force leading the country. Such a request was a *de facto* proposal to remove the monopoly power held by the party. When word of the proposal spread, the BBC, Voice of America and other news sources investigated and interviewed many of the "72." Without Internet, the chance to voice an opinion within and outside of the country would have been impossible.

But perhaps the most striking idea to us comes from our *Wall Street Journal* friend—Nguyên Pham Muoi. He has said that if one thinks deeply, Vietnam's history has created at least two Vietnamese economies: one domestic, the other international. By international, he means the millions of Viêt Kiêu who are now doing well in developed economies and are starting to invest or send financial support back to Vietnam. Muoi believes that there could be a "joint project" of building the future Vietnam, which could help solve temporary problems at lower costs and in a less time-consuming way. We agree with him. Revamping the economy to a state of burgeoning 9-10% growth rate is nothing other than reinventing a country; and Muoi's two Vietnams can do it much better than one.

Think About It: *What other ways could countries reinvent themselves?*

*

*   *

As Chiên's comment earlier in this chapter suggests, a country can be like a man, going through stages where each one is a chance to learn and change. That is what we've seen with Vietnam's relationships with the outside world. Vietnam's relationships with other countries have been fraught with emotion and skepticism, to be sure. After years of domination by China, by France, by the U.S., after a long dependence with the (former) Soviet Union that collapsed in the late 1980s, and after wars with neighbors over the last many decades, the country must be circumspect about who it works with. Indeed, in a *Wall Street Journal* interview before his July 2013 visit to the U.S., President Truong Tan Sang said, "We have time and again reiterated that Vietnam would not ally itself with one country to counter another." Indeed, the relationships that Vietnam has had, especially with foreigners, has followed a some common patterns.[14]

In the 1990s, the Vietnamese recognized that they needed to do business with countries outside the communist bloc, given the Soviet Union's slide and the lack of economic progress with countries like North Korea, Laos and Cuba. Although China was one example to watch, Vietnam's touchy relationship with it forced the Vietnamese to look elsewhere to learn. Thus, during the early stages of interaction with foreigners, the relationship was one of "foreigners as all knowing," with information from the outside world and ways of thinking that the Vietnamese wanted to learn. After a few years, that gave way to a hunger for understanding *why* the concepts and knowledge worked (or did not) and how they could be adapted for Vietnam.

But then came conflict. Once the Vietnamese felt they had learned (enough) from the foreigners, the attitude was "you have taught us all you can, give us the money and leave." Making the shift on both sides, from "teacher-learner" to colleagues and partner, was challenging. First, the foreigners had to recognize that their Vietnamese colleagues were fast becoming as knowledgeable as the foreigners

---

[14] Nancy K. Napier and David C. Thomas (2004). *Managing relationships in transition economies.* Greenwood Publishing Group.

themselves. That can be difficult for people used to being the "revered teacher," unquestioned by adoring students. Coupled with that mindset change was the recognition that the relationship was no longer one directional, from the foreigners to the local Vietnamese. Instead, it became a bi-directional and then a reverse relationship, where foreigners could learn much from their Vietnamese counterparts and bring that back to their own countries. At that point, the groups became equal partners.

In Nancy's case of working closely with Vietnamese, those four stages took at least seven years to complete. On the other hand, to shift from being passive in a planned economy mode to taking more responsibility for one's career and life and ultimately, for the country, and to do so in two decades says much about the ability to reinvent that we notice time and again in Vietnamese.

 Think About It: *When and how have you had to make a major shift in your thinking about another person or group of people? How did you do it? What helped, what hindered the process?*

*

*　　*

The Bridge Generation

We are hopeful about Vietnam for many reasons—the resourcefulness, resilience, and reinvention that so epitomize the people. We see that in the bridge generation, to be sure, but we also see something else. This group of people, born in the mid-1960s to late 1970s, is certainly not the first to have experienced the hardships and sadness of one or more wars, to have experienced serious famine, to have gone through shifts in political and some economic approaches. But it is the first generation of Vietnamese ever to have gone from essentially a way of life that the country lived for thousands of years to something that matches much of the world, and to do it in their own lifespan. To adapt to so much turmoil, technological, economic, and political change is unprecedented in the country. Those who have adapted, some who have thrived, are not the whole population of that age group, to be sure. But some have done very well and are emerging into leadership positions—in business, the arts, journalism and government.

In this last segment of the book, we'll offer examples of some and key lessons we have learned from them. First, they are the first group who have themselves—and increasingly their children—become global citizens as capable and driven as any others elsewhere. Second, they have repeatedly found themselves in situations—or explicitly put themselves into situations—that forces them to question themselves, their country, and their assumptions. Finally, some are beginning to lay groundwork for ideas that could shake the world. Let's look at three of the bridge generation who are making a difference.

*

*　　　*

Forty-year-old Bach Ngoc Chiên looks like a wrestler, with a no-nonsense body. Most Vietnamese men are rather slight, but Chiên is a solid man with a big personality. He's not overly muscular or threatening, but you still might give him a wide berth on the sidewalk simply because of his bearing. His face is square and the outsides of his eyes droop when he smiles. Like most executives connected to the world and serious about their work, Chiên places his mobile phone on the glass topped coffee table in his office and sneaks glimpses at it when it vibrates with an incoming call. He seems alert to the possibility that what he has and can change in an instant.

Chiên is the Director of VTV4, Vietnam's government owned television channel that broke ground in ways impossible just 10 years ago. His station beams to more than 2 million Vietnamese living outside Vietnam—in the U.S. and around the world. The programs range from interviews with foreigners to features on how the disabled are moving into mainstream society within Vietnam. Some of those programs, like the one on the disabled people, are powerful in ways few Americans could understand. The disabled and mentally ill, street children, and abused women have long been disenfranchised groups within Vietnam. In the early 1990s, many were on the streets of Hanoi as beggars, often children working alone, mothers sitting on the streets holding infants in their arms, or old men or women with crooked backs. Today, none are visible. But instead of ignoring them, efforts have started to work with and manage the problem, in part because of programs like the ones that Chiên produces.

Before his daughters were born, Chiên lived and worked in the U.S. for two years. He had an A-1 visa at the time, and felt very much at home in the country. In fact, when he returned for a visit much later, still using his A-1 visa, an immigration officer said, "Welcome home."

"Even at the CVS drug store, they treated me like anyone else in the store, not like a foreigner."

Yet, as much as his daughters find living in America to be special, he reminds them that Vietnam is their home country, not the U.S., and to remember that in America, they are guests.   But he also reminds them that when American friends come to visit in Hanoi, his daughters must be the hosts.

For all of his modern connectedness, Chiên is also thoroughly steeped in tradition. Maybe because he is older, he finds himself thinking more about his family's history and past and wants his children to be sure they understand the importance. His extended family of 13 lives in cluster of houses in Mo Lao, a former farming village now surrounded by the encroachment of Hanoi from the north. Chiên is decidedly well off and in the last twenty years of relative peace, he's been part of reason why economic development has taken Vietnam by storm. But he never takes it for granted. On a recent visit to Cuba, he reconfirmed that he never wants to return to the earlier life that he or his country had. He wants to move forward.

"Cuba was like Vietnam was 35 years ago. Slow life, old cars, happy people. But they don't know the outside world and what they don't have. It pushed me to realize I don't ever want to go back to that. I don't want Vietnam to re-live that time."

But he will never forget what he went through as a child in a very poor family and respects what his parents and the country have gone through.

"My mother made me red shorts, with the yellow star," Chiên recalled. "It made my teacher unhappy. She prohibited me from wearing the shorts to the school." The national flag was not to be used for boys' shorts, no matter how poor the family might be. Chiên's family is no longer poor. When Chiên leaves his office in the headquarters building for VTV4, near the center of Hanoi, he drives 45 minutes in heavy traffic to his home. Chiên and his extended family, now 13 members strong, live in several houses on Thanh Binh Road, in Mo Lao, a former farming village swallowed up in the spill of Hanoi's population over the last 15 years.

The Nhuê River skirts the village and parallels Thanh Binh Road, which is lined with concrete buildings.

The family compound includes three houses, for his parents, their three grown sons and each of their families. Chiên's home reflects what he tries to achieve in his life, straddling many worlds as gracefully as he can. His house mixes both traditional and modern architectures. His immediate family lives in two distinctive cultures—Hanoi and Washington, D.C. In Vietnam, he lives with three generations, respecting his parents and their more traditional values and trying to understand and rear his children with traditional cultural values while adjusting to newer ways of thinking.

The red Chinese style lacquer altar in Chiên's house is three layers tall. The first layer is about the height of a seven-year-old, and the upper two layers stair step up on top of one another like a pyramid. Photos of his great grandparents sit at the highest level, while the altar's middle and lowest layers are covered with offerings of flowers, fruit, and incense as well as photos of relatives lost to illness or to war, like Chiên's two uncles, who were killed during the American War. On the left side of the altar are traditional Vietnamese heavy wooden settees and tea table, along with two ancient kettledrums.

"I am more Vietnamese than any Vietnamese," he says.

Chiên worries that younger people may not fully embrace the traditional values that have been so long a part of Vietnam. Children don't respect their elders in the same way or they don't understand the hardships that their parents and grandparents experienced.

"When my father gave a scolding to my nephew who was in second grade, he [the nephew] called the 113 police. He said on the phone, 'Police, please come. Grandfather is killing Tom [his nickname].'" This is the equivalent of a second grader phoning the 911 emergency number in the U.S., claiming that a grandparent was doing evil.

"When I told my daughter about the family's hardship experience, and that I had to walk to the school, she asked me 'Why did not grandfather buy a car?'" Chiên sat back and smiled.

"Educating your children is getting difficult nowadays." Spanning multiple worlds brings influences that previously were "outside." Chiên now worries about the balance of his traditional life with that of the future pulling his children.

*
* *

Mrs. Vo Hoa Binh, organic farmer, scientist, and increasingly a spokesperson for her father, General Vo Nguyên Giap, offers a complementary perspective. She talks about how her father taught her about the importance of the country and its people. Because she took those lessons so much to heart, she believes that the Vietnamese people trust her because she tries to think about the country, rather than herself. Her attitude: give first, rather than taking for yourself. Sounds like some of the other leaders we have met.

*
* *

Hoang Ngoc, the young soldier who followed his supervisor's orders to transport illegal furniture—and was caught—grew up to be a journalist. Along the way, he learned the skills for being a journalist, including questioning information he had always believed to be accurate. Ngoc's first "aha moment" related to the Vietnamese war against Cambodia. Most Vietnamese believed that Vietnamese troops saved the Cambodian people from the Khmer Rouge's horrendous genocide in 1978. But a team of journalists from the Netherlands, in describing the Cambodian War, used word of "invasion" in connection with the Vietnamese army's actions. When Ngoc read that description he challenged it, since all he had ever heard was that the Vietnamese had gone to Cambodia to save the people. Yet, the evidence from the Dutch journalists, and their decidedly anti-Vietnamese slant, forced him, for the first time, to think differently about the meaning of the Cambodian War.

On another occasion, Ngoc was working with an American journalist who was doing research in an effort to understand the lives of Vietnamese soldiers who had fought in the American War. As part of the research, Ngoc and the American visited the Hô Chi Minh Mausoleum, at Ba Dinh Square, a very sacred part of Hanoi. The square is the site where Hô Chi Minh declared independent for the country in 1945. The mausoleum, which houses Ho's body for most of the year except when he returns to Russia for repairs, dominates the square. Visitors to the mausoleum learn that they must show the utmost respect—no photos, no hands in pockets, no talking. The experience can be quite moving indeed.

Next to the Mausoleum is a Russian-built museum that celebrates Hô Chi Minh's life, with exhibits that highlight key times of his life, from his birth in 1890, through periods of work and travel all over the world, to his time in various prisons, and the several wars that Vietnam fought during his lifetime. Just beyond the museum sits a replica of the simple, small bamboo stilt house that Ho lived in. If anything, many people argue that the stilt house is all he would have wanted to show the simple man that he was. Indeed, some claim that Ho would be appalled at the grandeur of the mausoleum and museum in his honor.

After they visited the mausoleum, Ngoc took the American journalist to a Bia Hoi restaurant on Ngoc Ha Street, to right near the entrance of the mausoleum. Bia Hoi restaurants are outdoor restaurants, often with small chairs or stools and rickety tables, where fresh draft beer is served. The American journalist was shocked and asked Ngoc why the authorities allowed such a noisy restaurant to sit just next to the most solemn and sacred place in Hanoi. The question baffled Ngoc, who had never thought that the juxtaposition was unusual. He tried to give her a "politically correct" answer: "Hô Chi Minh is our [the Vietnamese people] great leader and a great man with an ordinary life. Uncle Ho, therefore, does not mind if a Bia Hoi restaurant serving hundreds or even thousands of ordinary Vietnamese people every day sits next to his house." The journalist may have accepted the answer but Ngoc didn't forget the question and began to consider just how disorganized his country might seem.

When they entered the Bia Hoi restaurant, two uniformed military officers asked what they would do in the restaurant, other than drink beer. Ngoc explained that the American was seeking to understand the lives of former soldiers and the officers introduced them to a retired man in the restaurant. The old man was a former Director of Military Logistics, but had never gone to war, and thus was not of interest to the journalist, who declined to interview him. The two young officers, who by this time had likely lost face with the former director, were not happy and insisted that the older man was a good person for an interview. "He used to be a Department Director."

Just as Ngoc found some of the foreign comments, questions and attitudes surprising, so too does he think foreigners find Vietnamese. For example, he thinks that foreigners do not understand how and why Vietnamese people agree to take action—or refuse to act. On one hand, a Vietnamese counterpart underestimates a challenge and thus over promises to a foreigner, suggesting that a project, an agreement, or a task is on the right track. Then a problem emerges. The Vietnamese response: blame someone else for unexpected results. He convinces the foreigner he has tried his best, but that others have created the problem, leaving the foreigner to be confused and feeling that he has been made a fool. On the other hand, sometimes the Vietnamese counterpart refuses to pursue an opportunity at all, making no promise, and insisting that the mission is impossible.

What do Vietnamese think about Americans?

Ngoc finds Americans to be the friendliest foreigners who visit Vietnam.

"It is easy to make friends with an American drinker in a Bia Hoi restaurant," Ngoc laughs. "But Vietnamese people are just too clever by half. They make a simple thing much complicated. That prevents foreigners from understanding the true Vietnamese."

Ngoc feels that the way Vietnamese interact with foreigners reveals one of the main weaknesses in the Vietnamese way of thinking: seeking fast gains without realizing that those gains may be ephemeral, not long lasting or deep. The clever Vietnamese who meets and works with a foreigner, then, goes after the short term, fast benefit for himself, essentially trying to take advantage of his new naïve foreign friend. The quick transaction, especially when the Vietnamese feels he has bested the foreigner, builds the Vietnamese person's confidence and belief that he understands foreigners and is able to deal with them. Alas, this false sense of confidence is misleading since it focuses on the short term, neglects the risk-return thinking, and doesn't build longer term relationships.

As Ngoc has come to know more international journalists, he has seen common themes in the topics they pursue. Two are democracy and human rights.

"My favorite answer is..." Ngoc stops talking for a while, then begins again. "When a society is obsessed by food and security, democracy and human rights are luxury goods." The answer, he thinks, satisfies the foreigners because they typically move on to other topics. He hopes that his answers, and perhaps more so his willingness to talk with Americans, will help to change attitudes of how foreigners approach Vietnamese people. But their questions often cause Ngoc to look for different answers himself.

Think About It: How have your ideas about Vietnam (or America) changed as you've read about some of the people in this book?

Responsible Creativity

> *No coffee. No Life.*
>
> Trung Nguyên Coffee Saying

We close with a short profile of one more bridge generation entrepreneur. Dang Lê Nguyên Vu is founder and Chairman of Trung Nguyên Coffee, Vietnam's largest coffee firm. He started his younger life as a medical student before returning to his "coffee dream project" in his own central highlands province of Dak Lak, eventually become a so-called "coffee king" of Trung Nguyên, which means either "the Middle of Tây Nguyên" or "the middle way" in Vietnamese. The firm now employs over 5,000 people in Vietnam and has over 1,000 cafés, and he's after more.

Vu's firm has helped Vietnam become one of the top coffee exporters in the world. He is the man who said Vietnam should set a target of $20 billion in exports when the total world production was not even at that level. But Vu has dreams when he claims that coffee awakens the mind and then fuels ideas.

He plans to enter the U.S. market, just as Starbucks has set up shop in Vietnam. Besides coffee, he is passionate about grey hounds, race horses, and ideas. He also wants to help develop and unleash the next generation of Vietnamese entrepreneurs. Spending time with him is like being around a drug—he never stops thinking and talking about big ideas and big dreams. And he very likely scares people because of it.

These days, Vu is pushing to increase awareness among Vietnamese young people that they have a personal responsibility for the nation's prosperity and sustainability. He does this through something he calls "coffee spirit," a mix of entrepreneurial spirit and creative ability—a "dual engine" for growth. He calls it "responsible creativity," and he means to use it as a way for Vietnam to become a leader in creativity and in sustainability, and in the process, build world harmony.

Not a small task, even for the coffee king. But as a bridge generation leader, he may well be up to the task.

Vu is fervent about coffee's role in achieving those dreams. Simply the act of coming together over coffee brings people together, encourages talk, and recharges the brain and the body. (Ah, the beauty of caffeine!) And if you start looking, indeed, you'll find coffee houses and people talking in them all over the world, from Vietnam to

Botswana, from Australia to Finland. They are places of exchange—gossip, knowledge and ideas.

But Vu pushes even further. For him, responsible creativity reflects a sort of yin and yang—just as a coffee bean and the brain have two sides. From the yang side comes motivation and creativity to develop business and entrepreneurship, important for Vietnam's economic development. From the yin side comes the motivation and creativity for building harmony and sustainability. Vu wants the idea of responsible creativity to spur Vietnam. As he says, "If we can build both elements, prosperity and harmony, maybe peace could be close behind."

Coffee stimulates the brain. The brain sparks ideas. Ideas mean life. Vietnam has all three.

And that's exactly why we have hope for Vietnam.

Vietnam Factsheet 2012

Location:	Between latitudes 8° and 24°N, and longitudes 102° and 110°E.
Area:	331,210 sq km
Coastline:	3,444 km
Land borders with:	China, Laos, Cambodia
Population (July 2013 est.):	92,477,857
Population below poverty line:	11.3%
Labor force:	49.18 million
Unemployment rate:	4.3%
GDP (official exchange rate):	$141.7 billion
GDP per capita (current US$):	$1,595.8
GDP Growth:	5%
GDP composition by sector:	Agriculture 21.6%; Industry 40.8%; Services 37.6%
Public debt:	48.2% of GDP
Budget deficit:	-5.2% of GDP
Inflation:	9.1%
Exports:	$114.3 billion
Imports:	$114.3 billion
Reserves of forex. and gold:	$23.88 billion
External debt:	$53.08 billion
Stock of FDI Inward:	$73.95 billion
Stock of FDI Outward (Q1.2013):	$15.5 billion

Acknowledgements

We have many people to thank from both of our countries who helped make this project happen.

First, we express our deep thanks to the interviewees, without whom the book had no chance to exist.

We also appreciate kind help and discussions with colleagues: Hildy Ayer, Nguyên Tô Hông Kông, Daniel van Houtte, Elizabeth McKetta, Nguyên Nhu Ngoc, Lê Thi Nga, Dolly Samson, Kirk Smith, Sully Taylor, and Angeli Weller.

Trân Tri Dung was especially helpful in all aspects of creation, writing, editing and production of the book.

Special thanks also to experts and colleagues whose discussions, questions and comments have benefited us in various ways:

George Friedman and Jennifer Richmond (Stratfor), Nguyên Trung Truc, Anya Schiffrin Stiglitz (Columbia University), Roland Schatz (Media Tenor), Junichi Mori (Kyoto University), Andre Farber (Universite Libre de Bruxelles), Loke Kiang Wong, Vu Quang Hôi (Bitexco), Dam Thanh Son and Ngô Bao Châu (University of Chicago), Trân Dinh Thiên (Vietnamese Academy of Social Sciences), Ian Timberlake (Agence France-Presse), Marianne Brown (Deutsche Presse-Agentur), Trân Si Chuong, Adam Fforde (the University of Melbourne).

For their help with the book production, cover design, review, and marketing, we thank Shanshan Bai, Linda Clark-Santos, Stephanie Chism, Mike Comesky, Daryl Jones, Pat Kilroy, Joanna Lui, Cheryl Maille, and Jesse McMullin.

Beyond this book, many people have been instrumental in helping me (Nancy) understand Vietnam better and giving me a chance to be part of a project that brought Vietnam and the U.S. just a little closer. The project was funded by the Swedish International Development Co-operation Agency (Sida) for seven years and USAID for two years. Some of the people, by no means all, who were instrumental for Nancy included Suzanne Hosley and Cameron McCullough, the National Economics University and NEU Business School faculty and staff, many of the foreign professors who worked with us on the Sida and USAID projects, including Don Baron, Marjorie Lyles, and Bill Scheela, and many Boise State administrators, including Daryl Jones, Bill Ruud, Bill Lathen, Stacy Pearson, Lynn Gabriel, and Stephanie Camarillo.

About the Authors

Nancy K. Napier is Professor of Strategy and Executive Director of the Centre for Creativity and Innovation at Boise State University (USA) and Adjunct Professor of International Business at Aalborg University (Denmark). She holds the Medal of Honor from Vietnam's Ministry of Education and Training, in part for her work managing Boise State's involvement in a nine-year $8.5 million capacity building project at the National Economics University (Hanoi, Vietnam).

Vuong Quan Hoang received an MBA from Boise State University, a PhD from the University of Brussels, is co-founder of the Hanoi-based DHVP Research & Consultancy, and also serves as researcher at Centre Emile Bernheim, Université Libre de Bruxelles (Belgium). He was awarded Vietnam's National Book Prize 2007 and National Journalism Prize 2010.

Made in the USA
San Bernardino, CA
21 July 2015